AF269326

Why You're Wrong

Diarmaid Ó Conaráin

Why You're Wrong

Copyright © Diarmaid Ó Conaráin 2018

Published by The Human Spirit Publishing 2018
Dublin, Ireland
www.TheHumanSpiritPublishing.com

ISBN 978-1-9993060-0-7

<u>Dedicated Sincerely To;</u>

My partner Morgan and my family. For listening to me talk incessantly on these subjects before I decided to stop talking and start writing. Thank you for your love and patience.

Also dedicated to Prescott, Sydney, Katie, Micha, Sadhbh, Clodagh, and my unborn son. So begins the labour in effort to leave you a better world than you were brought into.

Contents

Preface

The hypothesis behind this body of work is that should our coherence and cognitive ability be still in good order, many of today's issues can be worked through without the involvement of conflicting scientists, quarrelling academics, disingenuous politicians or the overwhelming shadow of our big brother governments and media outlets who seek to feed us our thoughts daily.

My approach will not be one of an academic or qualified nature. I will not broach these quandaries from the stance of having more education or knowledge on the subject. That would be to argue my point as an "argument from authority". This is a fallacy, as being educated in the currently accepted knowledge on a subject, is no guarantee you are best placed to understand or decide on the course of action on a newly emerging issue. History has proven it will often be the creative, wise and visionary among us who shape the direction we're heading, and not those who have become educated on what we know thus far. I give no reverence to the notion that due to an individual being qualified or officially educated in a field, that their opinion on a matter is an indisputable truth. I am not sure any of us should. Especially given we are in strange times of people with borderline identical qualifications arguing separate sides of an issue.

In the earliest days of contemplation, before natural philosophy became science itself, there was the notion that some things can be observed or contemplated to a conclusion others could reach, and no logical individual should dispute. This is the beginning of philosophy; of science, arguably of modern civilisation itself. The embracement and cultivation of higher thinking, and the benefits we would soon reap from such an investment. It was indeed proven that with extended contemplation or study, if a conclusion was not reached there were at the least, benefits to the knowledge of the thing being studied to be gained. With focused and extended consideration of a thing or issue, one cannot avoid additional insight drawn from contemplating the varying possibilities or points of view of that thing or issue.

Yet in an age where information is spreading further and faster than ever, many have taken to simply reading and reciting. Leaving those in their fields to do the mental work while we accept the results they present, and reiterate them to each other as fact. This will not do in modern society. Furthermore, in the age of confirmation bias, appeal to emotion over intellect, widespread media favouring of one side of an issue, and science's credibility of conclusion in question due to regularly conflicting studies and opinions. It has become increasingly important to reignite our critical brains, and no longer meekly accept what we are told by those who may well have their own bias or agenda.

Therefore, it is my intention to examine these issue's as was done in the times of antiquity, by making use of the higher thinking we each possess. In hopes we might without bickering over studies or surveys from either side reach a critical thinking based conclusion, by exercising that which separates us from all other known life. It is my firm belief that although there is certainly disagreement, in cases downright deception on these issues, it is nevertheless entirely possible for us to contemplate them to a conclusion.

It is my intention to contemplate these issue's with no appeal to emotion, or seeking for you as the reader to give my contemplation any extra weight, owed to an education or qualification. Imagine us instead contemplating the plausible "what ifs?", that might broaden our insight on these topics, from which we may form a more concrete understanding or opinion of the matter.

Throughout this text, you will see reoccurring themes and points, as many of these issues overlap in their ideological foundations. Although I will venture to avoid repetition, at times overlapping due to conflicts or correlations of ideology or narrative will be necessary. We will observe over the course of these chapters that many of these seemingly unrelated issues share common foundations upon which they have built their ideas. I intend to examine not only the structural integrity of these ideas, but the plausibility of their application, and whether their goals achievement is sufficient to warrant their proposed means. Although we will not refer to scientific studies or academic advice as many may see these as both confirmation bias and argument from authority. We will however, from a common-sense approach consider relevant historical examples, and refer to authors concerning philosophies or topics that are relative. As several of these movements could not be addressed appropriately without consideration for ground-level examples that have occurred, or relevant writings that should be considered.

Although this may seem like a dip in and out piece of work of separate chapters, I would hope readers will progress in the linear manner it was intended to be read. As chapters have been placed deliberately in the order they are in, to aid in the painting of the bigger picture that exists collectively. The final footnote I might add is I do not intend to create offence. I am simply exercising the freedom of thought to contemplate these issues as a sovereign mind, entitled to come to my conclusion, and encouraging that you do the same.

CHAPTER 1

Equality

The convolution with equality is so nuanced that it slips quietly under the radar of the majority, who are simply too busy to lend extreme thought to a notion so seemingly rhetorical and unerring. Surely only a genuine bigot or discriminator could believe we shouldn't strive for equality? Yet therein lies the subtle chaos sprawling out before our very eyes. For having equal rights, and being equal, are quite different things.

Firstly, I would like to be clear, it is not my intention to discuss the extensive subject of equality in its entirety. To do so would require a larger text and lead us away from the overall point I would like to make regarding the connections between these topics. Therefore, I will discuss equality relative to its current iteration and movement. We will contemplate what it is and indeed what it isn't, that we might resolve its ambiguity. I may reference seemingly non-related aspects of equality, but merely to highlight their position relative to the current movement, to gauge where on the scales of extremity the current movement sits relative to all other writings.

Equality

Let us examine the word in question which has brought about so much friction, equality. Are we all equal? Surely the conversation must begin here. While we should all be entitled to equal rights, I am sure few would assert that we are equal. Regularly records are set in all manner of human achievement, by individuals whose success may never be matched again. In reality, it is not a difficult task to conclude we are not equal; we are individuals. There is not a single system of measurement or quantification in existence by which we're equal. The very definition of the word is an antithesis to the concept of individuality.

Why then is it we persist with the notion of equality? The implication surely being equality alludes to being equal in the eyes of society and the law; or having equal rights as it is more commonly put. Equal rights pertain to the notion that no legislation written accommodates one group that does not also accommodate all other groups. I would at this point hope that people embrace the reality of that notion. That for there to be an inequality of rights, we must be able to highlight a law or piece of legislation that expressly favours a particular group. Whether we base the group identity on gender, religion, social class or another form is irrelevant. One clear example of this is gay marriage rights, which thankfully most countries in western civilisation are moving towards policy change regarding this discrimination. Given the times of progression and information sharing we are in, it seems rhetorical that were there any other laws, pieces of legislation or rights such as this in existence, it would have been shouted from the rooftops by some form of independent or major media by now.

So why is everyone talking about equality? I believe it is chiefly that most are being agitated into action by the repeating aimless accusation that inequality exists, hence we must strive for equality.

We have seen that we enjoy equal rights, by virtue of there being no legislation to prove otherwise aside from same-sex marriage, suggesting we have an equal opportunity by law. The other society based factors such as bias, discrimination or social class through parenthood, need to be proved as systematic or institutional oppression of citizens, before they may be deemed as an inequality of rights. Since there is no policy, legislation or promotion of such bias or discrimination we can point to, we must conclude that these are the actions of individuals, and do not constitute a systematic or institutional movement aligned with the actions of the perpetrators.

Even in an attempt to level the financial situations in a community, there remain factors beyond control that will influence the outcome. One such example might be that one set of parents encourage and nurture their child, and tell them to work hard toward their dreams. While another set of parents might be neglectful or worse, abusive toward their child. No doubt instilling potentially damaging complexes to that child's ability to strive for what they want, while avoiding feelings of inadequacy.

Then we find natural aptitude, ability and individual factors to be taken into account. For instance, an eighteen-year-old who is 6ft tall and athletic, has a better chance at becoming a professional athlete when compared to the average male of that age. Few would argue that point, and we can attribute this to the genetic lottery where some are natural athletes, some naturally genius or artistic. Yet nothing can be done by any government or civil rights movement to level these contributing factors, to ensure equality of opportunity in these situations. Nor should it be, as that would be a move toward shunning individuality. We do not view it as an oppression that those who are not gifted athletically be superseded on the ladder of success in that field, by those more naturally athletic. We consider it the natural order, that the most talented or competent in a field, be the ones thriving in that field.

Where is the merit in insisting we are equal? When common sense proves otherwise, and when that false presumption leads to dangerous policy that advocates for redistribution, quota systems and judges society regarding figures aimed toward equity and nothing else.

These days people might say there is bias, even blatant discrimination in some industries or sectors of the workplace. I acknowledge this to be true in places, yet there is no legislation or law; creating, enticing or supporting such conduct. This, unfortunately, is merely reprehensible behaviour perpetrated by indecent individuals, who have found themselves in a position of power or influence. It does not qualify as systematic, as we cannot point to a single element of the system which encourages this behaviour. In fact, this bias now goes both ways, as in truth I am just as likely to be denied a job for being male by a female employer, who would rather see a fellow female receive the opportunity. To deny this growing inequality of insurance companies, start-up funds, etc., who specifically cater to women only is to be unaware or unwilling to acknowledge the sexism operating under the guise of creating equality. Equality will not be achieved by creating insurance companies that cater to women only. That is arguably sexist and exclusive in nature. It can be achieved by ensuring companies do not differentiate in the premium price, solely based on gender. Which in truth they do, as young men are statistically proven to be the most dangerous group on the road. Hence they receive the highest premiums and all are presumed to be a higher risk driver, based solely on data quantified by sex and age. So indeed it appears insurance companies have no problem applying gender-based generalisations to their business policy.

There exist many claims of differences between life for men and women, or people of different races, yet none of them equate to an inequality of rights. If a good looking woman is being approached regularly by men in public, she has every right to tell them to leave her alone, if they persist she can call the police for a case of harassment. Should this happen it is rhetorically wrong, and terrible behaviour on that particular man's part, yet no discrepancy between rights has occurred. A man approached a woman as happens every day of the week. When she tells him she's not interested, it is not out of a male-only right or entitlement that he believes he can persist and harass. He wrongly believes by persisting he might win her over, without realising he is pushing her further away. Yet again nothing here displays an advantage to either side in rights. The man is clearly committing the crime of harassment, and the woman has the right to call the police and have the situation reported and acted upon. It is unfortunate that incidents such as this example occur at any rate. Yet crimes of all natures are taking place every day of the week, they are not indicative of inferior rights of their victims, nor are they an indication of superior or extra rights held by the criminal. They are simply crimes that occur like any other, and the precise reason we have laws that address them specifically. For example, if there were no laws referring to sexual harassment whatsoever, this would be a blatant red flag signalling a society that is misogynistic and victimises one of its genders. However, the very fact that these laws exist to allow women to reprimand men legally for their actions, prove beyond doubt that not only does society not condone these men's actions, but it has taken steps to deter, criminalise and punish those who perpetrate such actions. Sexual harassment laws are also not exclusive to the female gender, thus not creating an inequality of rights. Ensuring that although instances of a woman sexually harassing a man are far lower, it has nonetheless not been overlooked by the law, as again the crime of sexual harassment protects all citizens equally.

With everything considered we should conclude that in western nations at least and leaving aside the concluding issue of gay marriage, we do enjoy equal rights. I see no merit in speaking on countries who have yet to develop their human rights to the extent that both sexes have equal rights. I consider it overly rhetorical and at least some of those countries have shown they agree by taking steps toward change. With Saudi Arabia, for example, women are now permitted to drive. With our own nations, they afford no right to one group over another, except for the right of marriage for the homosexual community. I see no merit in addressing this point as mentioned before I believe it to be rhetorical and most western governments are moving toward rectifying this inequality. With that being said, and leaving aside the developing issue of transgender rights, I believe nothing else in western countries can be pointed to as proof of any one group having rights that another group does not. Some may argue there is bias, people in power who are perhaps sexist or racist, or even systematic misogyny or racism. Yet there is no legislation supporting such accusations, or behaviour to highlight or equate to unequal rights. The reality being those people being employed is not proof that the system encouraged their behaviour, nor is it proof the system somehow operates in the same manner as those individuals, or that it is company policy. Leaving accusations of a patriarchy or systematic racism flat-footed, as they fail to find a single piece of legislation or right that will substantiate their claim.

It is correct that we should enjoy equal rights, but common sense disproves any notion of being equal, by any definition of the word. Even leaving aside naturally attributed distinctions and nurture acquired differences, there will also be personality variance; some more organised than others, some more motivated, some more resourceful, and on and on our differences build and build, until we arrive at the conclusion reached in western society many years ago. That we are indeed individuals, a thing we should continue to embrace, value and protect. To wrongly promote equality is to encourage and value the idea of sameness, which in turn serves to ostracise the concept of the individual. Though individuals may enjoy equal rights, making them equal in the eyes of society and the law, they can never be literally equal, and to be so would erase their individuality.

Then with citizens in western nations enjoying equality in the eyes of the law in today's societies why is there still so much attention and drive being given to the notion of equality? I would argue it is because the movement is not what most believe it to be. As the chief concern of the movement of equality is not rights or opportunity, but the outcome.

Equality of opportunity versus equality of outcome is a very important issue, that is being silently fought over in an under the table manner. It would appear none who believe in equality of outcome will openly state it, for fear the public will largely disagree and they will lose their political standing. Instead, they quietly push for the policy that is acutely designed and shaped to move towards the equality of outcome they seek. It has long been the goal of democratic societies to provide equality of opportunity for every citizen, in so far as was possible. Yet equality of outcome is an idea that has never been realised and is entirely different in its aims and philosophy. Let us briefly discuss their differences for the benefit of readers unfamiliar with the terms.

Equality of opportunity pertains to the notion that we should all enjoy an equal chance, as it were, at achieving any career choice we should desire. Although we have seen true equality of opportunity is virtually impossible to achieve, due to the many natural variables, it is then systematic equality of opportunity that concerns us. Whether the system and society we live in affords each individual a systematic equal opportunity. The working life of most in the modern day will be that of a trade, college, entrepreneur or what we might label a job, being a position that individuals with no qualifications can hold. Barring acts of bias or prejudice, no systematic advantage is given to any group when applying for an apprenticeship in a trade. This equates to equal opportunity in these industries, as nothing about the process of these systems can be deemed to give any group an advantage over the other. Isolated events of discrimination may occur but as mentioned these are individuals actions and not a policy of any kind. As entrepreneurs individuals enjoy intellectual property rights to any of their creations, all are entitled to form a business or create a product at any time, displaying no inequality of opportunity. Anyone pursuing this route will quickly find start-up capital is their main issue, yet all entrepreneurs struggle with this aspect, and there is nothing systematic or discriminatory in the matter of people not having the money they desire to start a business. There may be a discrepancy between social classes and the ease of entering business, this is attributed to cumulative family wealth. While entire class systems have been formed and do indeed influence opportunity, each individual in each class is arguably there due to cumulative generational family success. Again with jobs, leaving aside individual acts of reprehensible behaviour, no advantage is afforded one group over another in the selection process from a systematic or policy standpoint. Leaving us lastly with college, which aside from a nation or two in western civilisation, again there is no systematic advantage afforded any group. I reference in particular the United States of America as one of the few places where group identity holds weight. As affirmative action has over-run actual equality of opportunity in universities, and replaced it with an inequality aimed at Caucasian and East Asian students. Most are familiar with affirmative action, few consider for very long that it is discrimination, as admitted openly by its labelling as positive discrimination. To afford certain groups bonus points on the SAT exam should be seen as nothing but discrimination, there is nothing positive about it. Or are we to imagine we might someday enjoy positive sexual assault? Or positive racism and positive theft? As the South African government no doubt wrongly view their theft without compensation of land is a form of positive discrimination, I am inclined to strongly disagree. Similarly, for many professions in Germany their states sexist policy asserts that should both a man and a woman be equally qualified for a position, the employer must award the position to the female. This policy seeks to increase the representation of women in the workforce, yet is again undeniably sexist in its nature and application. Leaving aside the isolated examples of inequality and discrimination mentioned, we enjoy equality of systematic opportunity in western nations.

Equality of outcome, however, is an entirely separate concept, with a very different aim in mind. The advocates of this policy argue the only reason there are those against it, is due to being raised and conditioned by a capitalistic society, or worse, because we have something to lose in the transition. The latter simply does not apply to the majority of people. The former critique is not entirely untrue, though it disregards the overwhelming fact that we live in capitalistic societies precisely because we've agreed, for the most part, in its ideals and mode of operation. Equality of outcome states that any unequal distribution of positions of employment or wealth is unquestionably a direct indicator of oppression or discrimination. Its assertion is that in a just society, we would find equal numbers of sexes and races across all industries. This is isolated idealism, removed from the reality of human nature. It also shares the short-sighted idealism of Marxism, as its conclusions are entirely speculative and ignorant of organic developments, the Pareto distribution theory being one. To truly demonstrate its policy and thinking I believe will require examples. Equality of outcome states in any class or field of study there should be equal representation. That is to say, unless a physics class has an equal number of men and women, then sexism is clearly present. If there isn't an equal percentage of each race in the class, then racism is present. This theory applies to all classes, professions or fields of study. It is certainly worth noting equality of outcomes position on the scales of extremity. In the sense that of the theories and writings on equality, even the vast majority of communists do not advocate for such an extreme result. Consideration of its principle relative to other ideas, presents equality of outcome as the most extreme and polarised belief in the field of equality.

Most I believe would agree that this shows absolutely no consideration for human nature. Is it not more likely that beautician and makeup artists are predominantly female professions? Or that perhaps the college field may be unbalanced to begin with, due to the relatively large number of males who might undertake an apprenticeship for example. It is overly idealistic to imagine that millions of individuals will divide themselves organically into neatly equal representative boxes. Equality of outcome is a fallacy as it will inevitably, in the name of achieving its goal, force people away from their natural interests in serving the purpose of achieving true equality of outcome. It is a narrow-minded, wilfully ignorant principle, that seeks to reshape the workplace of humanity, by virtue of eventually introducing gender and race quotas. Which will have chilling effects on society, when women find themselves afforded 50% of the bin collecting jobs, or half of the industrial plumbing positions. While men who lack the preferred disposition potentially end up caring for the elderly or children. Countless circumstances can be highlighted to demonstrate equality of outcomes failings as a philosophy, and to my knowledge (as I do not claim to have read everything written) of the great minds of history who have written on equality and justice, none who we regard as household names have supported equality of outcome. From Plato to Descartes to Marx, many have nuanced views on equality, yet none saw equality of outcome as a plausible idea, not even communists.

The danger of destroying the value of individuality, cannot be overstated. Preaching that we are the same is not only incorrect, it actively discourages progression and evolution in society. Where would Tesla have found his idealistic audacity to believe he could invent the alternating current? Had he been bullied into the idea his whole life, that he was exactly like everyone around him, and thinking otherwise was not only incorrect but was offensive to others. This peer pressure of political correctness serves to discourage individual innovation, which only serves to deprive the world of the many things brought to us by individuals, or small groups of people.

The only solid conclusion we can draw is that certainly important positions are held by those who should not have them, and those with power or influence by mandate of their position must be watched closely to ensure there is no personal bias leading to direct abuse of power.

Though it is never seen as an oppression of men that there are many women making a living from modelling, with many even becoming celebrities in their own right. Men rhetorically buy clothes too, yet either we are not considered worth marketing to or they believe it would be to no avail. It is clear when pointed out that far more resources are used advertising to women, which in turn leads to far more modelling jobs being available to women. Since the days of Cindy Crawford women have been supermodels, not only worthy of global fame, but often accessing other industries later, such as acting or business in the form of clothing or perfume. These are, for the most part, opportunities that are not afforded to men. Or I challenge the reader to consider how many men that started as models they can name, who then had the success of say, Naomi Campbell, Tara banks or Cindy Crawford. Yet as highlighted we do not see this as proof of a conspiring matriarchy. Or that women are keeping the good jobs with the ladders to the top for themselves. Nonsense, it is simply the evolving market structure, demand controls which direction a thing moves, and in this case the modelling industry simply gravitated naturally toward women from a marketing standpoint.

Then there are positional goods to be considered relative to equality of opportunity. As discussed by Adam Swift in his book, Political Philosophy, positional goods can create an inequality. To give an example of a positional good, he gives the example of private healthcare. His conclusion is that private healthcare may be an inequality to many, yet it does not serve to lessen the service received by those in public healthcare. If anything, the fact thousands of individuals now purchase private healthcare, will serve to lessen the strain on the public sector, hence potentially improving the public sector service or efficiency. Often the aim of equality in discussion or policy is to raise the bar, so to speak, for those in society who are the worst off. Whereas Swift outlines that private education earns the title of a positional good in a more literal sense. This arises attributed to the general practise that for many employers a degree from Harvard is more favourable than many other colleges or universities. A third level education from a state college may be equivalent to that of a private one, yet when seeking employment there is a distinct possibility that one is favoured over the other, thus applying a positional value. Since this alleged added value is based solely on location of study, and location of study can be almost entirely attributed to financial circumstances, Swift concludes that for this reason it is a less tolerable inequality than private healthcare. As we see many working-class students are denied the opportunity to acquire this alleged added value education as they lack the finances to attend private facilities.

However, private healthcare may indeed lower the standard of service to the public, as the best doctors and surgeons are head-hunted by the private sector. This, of course, is a rational move on the private sectors behalf, as they seek to provide a service warranting the additional cost. Though for a public sector potentially unable to compete financially for the most talented surgeons, a lowering of standards may well be the outcome. Perhaps leading to the conclusion that the state might supplement the cost of the most complex surgeries in private facilities for public sector members, thus ensuring equality of service for all when warranted. It is not my intention to resolve every facet of equality in this chapter, but to illustrate that many issues are deeply complex with no simple solution. One might suggest simply abolishing private healthcare. The outcome of this may inevitably be undue pressure on the public system, and also a similar situation to the point I will now make regarding private education.

Let us examine the motivation behind private education, as this may be pertinent to our understanding and acceptance, or lack thereof of such an inequality. Private education began no doubt as many capitalistic ventures begin, with the idea that certain individuals perform tasks at a higher level than others, and that might be considered more valuable. The task in this case is teaching, and I believe few would doubt that like in any other profession, there are individuals who are far better at teaching people new things than others are. It seems private education sought to acquire and consolidate the talents of the more competent professors, and offer them to the public marketed as a higher standard for a higher price. This occurs in many industries, yet my having a car worth 150 thousand dollars does not serve to offer me additional employment opportunities, as a private education might. To this extent we may dismiss many other examples of varying standards for varying prices. Professors and academics of course did not resist the idea of private education, and why would they? Who turns down the prospect of earning a higher wage for performing the same task? In truth then private education can only be labelled as a natural occurrence and not an intended oppression or inequality. Individuals will always seek to repackage products for a higher price, to sell to those who can afford it. Were this not the case companies like Ferrari might have never existed, knowing they would never have millions of sales per year, as the general public is not their intended consumer base.

It is my own belief that private education as a positional good, although creating inequality, is not something that should be abolished. Often in discussing equality the expressed aim is that of raising the standard of living for those who are considered the worst off in society, dragging up the average so to speak. I believe private education facilitates that goal, as students attending private facilities are not holding spaces in public facilities. Meaning the more students who pursue private education, the more students who can pursue a third level education overall. As mentioned, this satisfies the criteria of raising the average, as presumably more open slots at public facilities, will equate to more people studying. Many may argue this may be achieved by simply adding to the number of public facilities in the first place, and abolishing the private ones with the aim of eradicating the inequality created. Yet I would argue that this infringes of the rights of individuals in unacceptable ways. Consider that abolishing private education facilities leaving only state run organisations is tantamount to endorsing a government monopoly, in which the state tells its citizens you may never enter business in this industry as it belongs to us. I believe it will also serve to put a roof on earnings for professors and academics, as there is often very little variance or inflation on the earnings of civil servants. This may well discourage students from entering a field which most would agree could very much benefit from enticing our best and brightest, to continue teaching our next generations.

I also believe that the inequality spoken of is not quite so overbearing a factor as it may be presented as. Consider that when multiple individuals with similar qualifications apply for a position, the employer is forced to find a reason why one candidate is favourable to another, given they share similar qualifications and someone must be chosen. Often where the qualification was acquired can be the determining factor, yet just as often, personality will be that deciding factor. As employers are as likely, if not more so, to employ amicable and personable staff, as they are to select a candidate based on the reputation of the facility they studied at.

Lastly with this issue and those like it in respect to positional goods, as pointed out with aptitude or talent, some natural factors may never be made entirely equal. If we were to abolish private education, we will still find some more adept at teaching than others, hence arguably some students might receive a better education, regardless. The inequality of which students earn the privilege of being taught by the best professors will simply settle itself in non-financial ways. For example, it may become known that one facility has a particularly excellent engineering professor, hence would-be engineering students frantically apply for entry to that facility. Of course there will be a limited amount of places so only a select few will be taught under this professor, leading us to the conclusion that education can never be entirely equal. Though I agree it is not a matter that should be settled financially, but in a manner most would agree is most deserving. That is to say that entry to Harvard or institutes like it should not be dependent on financial circumstances, but rather positions allocated by virtue of performance. An example being that perhaps private facilities should accept students based on their test scores alone, ensuring the limited number of positions available go to the most deserving and hard-working students. If there were fifty places available perhaps they should go to the fifty highest scoring applicants. The only way to facilitate this would be for the state to finance students who are unable to afford the private facilities services, ensuring that having the highest test scores would be sufficient to secure your place. This would ensure that intellect is rewarded over capital in the field of education. Though as highlighted, intellect is subject largely to the genetic lottery. The issue will then arise of those who have paid for the facility feeling there is an inequality, due to some having been supplemented by the state. However this is arguably the kind of inequality that can lead to pulling the overall average higher, so perhaps it should be permitted. Of course the simpler solution would be to encourage employers to cease providing favourable bias to students who received private educations. Yet as I have mentioned, an employer is forced to find a determining factor on who to employ from the many similar applicants. To force them to ignore the potentially differing standards of qualification, is arguably to prevent them seeking out the most competent or well qualified employees for the job, which I do not believe the state has the right to do.

Housing I believe should be given consideration as a positional good given development trends of nations and societies as a whole. This would be housing with respect to location, and not size or value of the property. In fact we find that housing as a positional good directly ties in with both prior positional goods. For example, living in a rural area compared to living in a city. Firstly in a rural area you may not have access to private healthcare locally, and it is likely for healthcare issues most would rather avoid excessive necessary travel to avail of such a service. Secondly, in remote or more rural areas it is likely there exists little or no private education. This not only leaves you at the obvious disadvantage of not being able to enjoy private education without moving away from where you live. It also presents housing as a positional good more directly. As the rural student now faces accommodation costs in a new city which will be higher than their previous rural costs, to attempt to compete for private education. Whereas those students born and living in a city are likely to be afforded the opportunity to attend private facilities while living at home, thus incurring no financial burden as the rural student will. Few would argue that student debts are currently too high already, and we will likely see fewer rural students each year capable of footing the high bill of accommodation in the city while unable to work full-time. In a manner similar to the above circumstances housing can prove itself a positional good with regard to opportunity also. Consider that to open a convenience store or perhaps a mechanics garage in a rural area will prove difficult, in terms of guaranteeing sufficient revenue to allow a business to be sustainable. Whereas in a city with likely millions of people the opportunity for potential business is far higher merely by virtue of the population. It can of course be argued as relative, with costs to start a business in a city being much higher to begin with, while also facing what is likely far more competition. To this extent we might conclude that the variants somewhat cancel each other out, and in truth it proves equally tough in rural or city settings to succeed in business. Though each issue will prove to be individual and circumstantial, let us examine the convenience store model more closely for a moment. Consider the known fact that purchasing in bulk achieves a lower price per unit. Since the rural convenience store is likely to have a lower turnover, they cannot buy many items in large bulk as they would simply go out of date. They may also pay a higher price for delivery of goods due to the distance from the supplier, or they also pay a higher price for goods due to it being a smaller rural supplier, who cannot purchase similar bulk quantities to the major supermarket chain suppliers. This translates into less of a profit margin for the rural convenience store when compared to one in a city. Which many will testify translates into higher priced products for consumers in rural areas. It is not uncommon for individuals in rural areas to find themselves paying two to four times the price for basic necessity goods when compared to inhabitants of cities. One might argue population growth will inevitably raise opportunity in a given rural area. Though in reality population growth struggles in these areas, specifically due to opportunity and education as each generation sees individuals move to cities for employment.

It is also likely that rural dwellers find themselves suffering lower standards of service from an array of modern luxuries. For example in more isolated rural areas not only will phone service or Wi-Fi be badly functioning, but they may find themselves facing extortionate rates for services such as home heating. Companies justify this through the necessity to turn a profit in less valuable regions, while often times holding a monopoly over areas undesired by their competition, further facilitating extortion of communities with virtually no choice. Issues such as barely functioning or indeed non-existent Wi-Fi, can also prove to be an inhibiting factor on opportunity. Every year individuals pursue further education online, along with the rapidly expanding necessity of many individuals and business' to have access to the internet on a daily basis. This lack of basic service delivery when considered relative to a cities performance in the same industry can surely be considered an inequality, as in the modern day internet access or the lack thereof, serves to facilitate or stunt growth and opportunity. Many more examples such as road quality, entertainment and recreational facilities or public transport could be discussed, but as mentioned earlier it is not my intention to delve completely into equality. Indeed many may cite the disadvantages of living in a city such as housing costs or pollution, but I believe for the most part I have demonstrated that rural areas are subject to neglect by the private sector and systematically by the state. This serves to at minimum confirm that regardless of which way the scales tip, housing is indeed a matter to be considered regarding equality and more specifically positional goods.

Alas we must conclude this is not the concern of the current movement for equality either, as if any of the above are mentioned it is solely education, and never in a solution based manner other than to eradicate private education entirely. Which I believe we have shown will not solve inequality and serves to lower the standard for all involved in multiple ways. Again I believe we must conclude this movement is nothing but a push for equality of outcome, and further demonstrations in later chapters will serve to strengthen that summation. Moreover I believe we have proven that its aims are quite selective also, as it disregards many true inequalities, so it might march forward with its agenda. In truth it would appear many western governments are facilitating the perpetual rise of urban housing prices, to the benefit of the banking industry, further demonstrating their indifference to inequalities that do not serve their narrative.

Equal representation might be considered the final topic of equality regarding the current movement, but I will address this later in the Gender & Race Quota chapter.

In conclusion, we arrive at the haunting prospect that seen as the field can never truly be levelled, the only way to ensure societal equality of outcome is to prevent citizens aspiring or climbing higher than the lowest capabilities. For fear it might inevitably lead to inequality, which would become indicative of oppression. Since we cannot all climb to the same height, the only equality can be for us to remain on the ground alongside each other. This may appear to be an extreme shaping of the issue, but I assure you there is nowhere else for this ideology to lead but to this conclusion. If inequality is to be eradicated, there are virtually no ways to achieve this other than to suppress those attempting to rise beyond the average.

CHAPTER 2

Diversity

As I believe we have seen we are not equal, perhaps now is the correct time to speak on the rapidly gaining momentum thesis of diversity. Of course, diversity would be entirely unnecessary were we all equal, though the advocates of diversity seemingly agree with my conclusion that we are not identical, hence diversity is to be valued, and strived for in their eyes. There are many among us who would advocate for diversity of representation and ideas, and again this seems like a borderline rhetorically sensible idea. Let us examine it nonetheless that we might come to a more than borderline conclusion on the matter.

It is, in essence, a progressive idea to observe a more varied pool of ideas and experiences will most likely yield better results than one made up of similar people, likely having similar ideas and experiences or outlooks. Not only in business is this idea being given serious consideration but also in other areas such as media or political representation. Again as a rule of thumb, one may find it hard to argue against such a seemingly just movement. Yet let us examine critically the proposed parameters to put in place such a system or quota.

It appears no matter what country the conversation is being had in, the presumption or indeed the policy of diversity is to be racially based. It seems unconcerned with the diversity of social class, a geographical perspective of urban to rural dwellers, or any other form of diversity, as it has its sights fixed firmly on racial diversity.

Let us examine whether the presumption that a diversity of ideas must be racially or culturally based has any merit to it, or whether the diversity of ideas desired might be achieved organically from within a given community or country. Although I agree we're not empirically equal, that is not to presume we're wildly different either, or that those differences stem from or can be solely attributed to race, gender or culture. To do so is making a presumption on millions of people based on race or gender, the very definition of racism and sexism to my eyes. It is hard to shape the notion that individuals from a different race, culture or country will innately be different or harbour different creative ideas, as anything other than presumption. In truth I would like to hear but cannot find a justification for this presumption or evidence it is based on, as evidence rarely seems part of the argument. Creativity I do not believe has any correlation to race, or indeed gender or nationality, and there are no studies to my knowledge which would advocate otherwise. It is a human trait bestowed upon individuals seemingly at random, as part of the genetic lottery. So then to assume a company functions better with the addition of diversity of race or culture, is in truth a fallacy. Slogans like "diversity is our strength" may be true in displaying togetherness and community, but have no relevance or pertinence to the success of a business. To imagine it would can only be diagnosed as wishful presumption. It is also ignorant of existing evidence, to imagine the fresh or unique ideas that a business seeks will not arise organically within a given community or country.

As the truth of humanity's progression for millennia before the idea of diversity stands as overwhelming proof. As individuals such as Socrates, DaVinci, Einstein, the Wright brothers and Gandhi were people with extraordinarily different ideas, that indeed shaped the future, and yet all were native to their country. None of them had come from other cultures or outside races which attributed to their success. Indeed history has more evidence attesting to similar examples to the above, than it has testifying to the notion of outside genius being imported. Some might argue cases like operation Paper clip lend proof to the opposing theory, but these were isolated uncommon events, and often arguably came from within incredibly similar cultures.

Seemingly the application of such an idea based on the established presumptuous criteria of race equating to diversity, is solely based on achieving diversity of race and culture, anywhere it is perceived to be lacking. It appears then the term diversity is being used somewhat deceptively, as those advocating for it rarely voice their true desire, which is specifically race-based inclusion or importation. As I have pointed out diversity is almost never discussed as a matter of social class, geographical in reference to urban or rural dwellers, or diversity of consumer base, or even diversity of fields of expertise. No, it would appear diversity wherever discussed is solely a racial movement, aimed at placing more non-indigenous people in what are perceived to be desirable, or hard to achieve positions in society.

The notion presumably must be then that diversity is necessary to overwhelm racism. Whether a systemic racism problem is the case or not will be examined in the chapter on racism. Though again I highlight, it is quite presumptuous to imagine that because there is a lack of a certain group in a workplace, then there must be racism afoot. This is a naive dividing of the world's population into a personally satisfying viewpoint of society. Many believe humanity should have divided itself up nicely in equal proportions among every trade, and there could be no natural interest factor causing discrepancies in employment ratios across varying industries. It can be difficult in earnest to take this view seriously when factoring in the varying demographics of individual countries. Not to mention the fact that qualified immigrants went to certain countries specifically because they knew nurses for example or builders were needed. These individuals saw an opportunity and potentially an economic boom and seized it. Often spurring more of the same to happen, thus organically creating misrepresentation in certain fields. This very often occurs naturally either way among classes. As we find the majority of trades will be occupied by the working class, whereas a lot of the solicitor, judge and TV presenters will come from the local upper class.

I put it to the reader that those concerned with diversity are in fact the people who see us as separate due to our race, or they would feel no need to ensure there was inclusion. They have a race-based view of the world, and compute everything they see by a personal measuring stick of equal numbers of colours distributed perfectly evenly. It may be inappropriate to call this actual racism, but it is unquestionably race-based decision making, which can only be seen as racisms ugly cousin. Similar to "positive" discrimination, race-based decision making even with a virtuous aim is still race-based decision making. This presumption also has defined itself a target. Again white men appear at the top of the totem pole in these individuals eyes as oppressors, and apparently, a collection of white men in an employment area is evidence of racism and sexism. Well, how nice of them to be truly racist and attribute broadly a terrible behavioural trait with an entire group of hundreds of millions of people. However the blind and baseless accusations are indeed sexist and racist in nature, the very things they accuse their victim of being. I say victim because every European man has been painted as oppressive in their very nature, this can be seen as nothing by rational individuals but a wild racist allegation.

As their assumption of whether certain behaviour is present or not is based purely on how many people of colour are in employment. This misguided viewpoint assumes non-Europeans even applied for positions in the first place. After all, an employer can only choose from his or her applicants. Or should we expect employers to chase diversity and come across intrusively, approaching random people of colour asking them would they like to be employed? Again I would point out how discriminating that would be, as employers target minorities to employ as a pawn on the board of diversity, equality and virtue signalling scales of social justice measurement. Colleges potentially doing the same would certainly make it much easier for minorities than the indigenous masses, who are left to fight it out according to our current model while minorities are headhunted so companies and colleges might fill their diversity quota.

It must be concluded it is racist in nature as a point of fact, to presume that simply because someone has a different skin colour or ethnicity, they somehow naturally harbour wildly different ideas to our own. To presume that someone from a different country or culture will be entirely different is essentially bigotry, even if the intended presumption is not one of bad judgement, it nonetheless is a presumption about an individual based on their race, culture or country of birth.

Contrary to this naive and somewhat innocent presumption, it is overwhelmingly likely the precise reason individuals emigrate to another country is specifically driven by their agreement and favouring of the system of the country they're moving to above their own. To be put another way, that they emigrate because their ideas align already with their new country, more so than their own. In essence it becomes a fallacy to presume their beliefs or ideas will be anything but highly similar to those already existing, and may well find themselves feeling uncomfortable and singled out when we presume they can share exceptionally different or valuable ideas. Imagine yourself having moved to China. In your first week at your new job while having a staff meeting your boss singles you out as their "diversity representative", and shines a spotlight on you in front of everyone to produce wildly diverse and original ideas. There are an amount of us who relish such an opportunity to be heard and give creative input. Yet the larger majority of us would feel singled out, and unjustly put under unfair pressure by comparison to every other staff member. We might even feel as though we had just experienced a form of prejudice, as we were singled out solely because of our different race or culture. Then expected to produce new ideas as if every individual from a race or culture is a representative for that race or culture. Again, horrendously presumptuous and ignorant, as we may find these individuals are not creative at all, or share no particular affinity with what we might presume to be their culture.

Why then the sudden push for Diversity? Is it simply well-meaning confusion, bias and naive presumptions? And why are the aims so skewed? For example that there be equal representation on a racial basis, despite the actual population percentage. Is it not madness to advocate what might be 5%, 12% or even 30% of the population should be afforded 50% of representative positions? Is this not precisely the kind of over-representation that gave rise to this movement in the first place?

The token black actor was often the complaint of many in reference to representation on-screen in the United States. That such a sizeable section of the population be expected to be satisfied with a singular representative so often on screen. This was challenged and rightly so, yet is it not equally ludicrous to imagine one-fifth of the population are represented on screen and in government as if they were half the population? Surely if anything this would now be tilting the balance of power wrongly to the extent of undermining the democratic principle that, each person's vote is equal? This principle is attacked when we discuss affording a section of the community more power than is warranted by the democratic principle.

It may not always be ideal but the fundamental principle of a democracy is that we're all afforded an equal vote, and in essence, majority rules. It is the government's obligation to ensure everyone's human rights are preserved, yet beyond that the democratic will of the people must be observed. The very idea of which is undermined if we afford certain groups more representation than is proportionately owed to them.

In fact, it runs completely contrary to the PC ideology that often promotes it. In the hypocritical sense that on the one hand the movement advocates we're equal, yet on the other hand insists on requiring "diversity" based solely on race and gender. One is left to wonder which ideology is to be supported, given diversity based on race or gender inclusion supposes not only can different ideas not come from within a single group but also that a separate group will presumably have different ideas to the previous group. This is of course in reference to the theory of a diversity of ideas which is sweeping the world, but being framed as a racial issue.

To a large extent I find it condescending that diversity be used as a measuring stick for how progressive or socially just a business is, marching out its non-indigenous pawns in a twisted display of self-virtue. Which then implies a lack of the former must also equate to a lack of justice, or more aptly described, the presence of racism or sexism. Which of course is nonsense if you consider theoretically, a hairdresser in a predominantly black neighbourhood in the United States of America being admonished for her discriminatory behaviour of having possibly only black employees. This is a completely presumptuous and twisted view, as perhaps the lady in question started the store with her sister, and as business sped up they took on their cousin too. Now let us imagine that one or all had daughters or other family members interested in joining the family business, and so they did. Now have the owners of the business employed discriminatory practises? I would argue they have not, there may be an argument for nepotism, but there was certainly no deliberate attempt or intent to prevent other races from attaining jobs there. It was merely a case of employers favouring the idea of having employees they can trust, have known for a long time and will get along with.

This is the major danger with the idea of equality of outcome. It is inherently indifferent towards the reality of human nature and in some cases utterly oblivious to real-world information. One example of equality of outcome is to propose, if a college course with 30 places exists, then those places should be filled equally in proportion to sex and race. That there should 5 white men and women, 5 black men and women, and 5 Asian men and women. This seems to be the formula regardless of racial proportions within the actual country, regardless of whether those ratios are actually interested in being in the class, and regardless of whether that proportion of people actually qualify for the course. It is imperceivable to the preachers of this idea that there could be a natural imbalance. That there might be more men naturally interested in mathematics and more women naturally interested in art. This occurrence in the eyes of equality of outcome is proof of oppression or discrimination, and must in turn be rectified. So now instead of individuals feeling there are jobs they can't do, there will be individuals being told there are jobs they must do, to fulfil the equality of outcome pie of distribution. And I put it to the reader that diversity is merely an offshoot component of the agenda of equality of outcome.

In summary, although I deeply agree with the proposition of a diversity of ideas and representation, I denounce the bigoted presumption this diversity should be, or could only be attained through racial importation or quotas, and I disagree with any movement seeking to distribute power or influence solely proportionately or unfairly. I acknowledge that with a diversity of ideas we increase our chances of progression, but I see no proof either empirical or historical that ensures this is a racial or cultural issue. I also agree that every group should have appropriate representation, but I believe that to be so restrictive in this policy as to distribute power and influence directly proportionately throughout groups, may well hinder the principle that the positions be filled by those best qualified and suited to the given position. As it may well do if we are to be so restrictive as to mandate proportional representation, over simply the merit of individuals suitability and competence. I propose that time and time again the notion of diversity will intrude on and obstruct the organic development and employment of individuals everywhere. It is certain racial or sexual discrimination cannot be tolerated, but I am equally certain that enforced diversity will not be the answer, as it is fixated solely on race. When what should be valued is a diversity of skills and personal traits, placing human individuality over a simple check-list of skin colour or country of origin.

Diversity of representation will be discussed further in the Gender/Race quota chapter coming next.

In closing there may be a lot to be said for the idea that a sample of something different is great, but a large percentage of it begins to change the norm. This may seem trivial but when the issues run deep culturally, ideologically or religiously, it can lead to great conflict within communities composed of the indigenous peoples of that land and the newly arrived migrants who have yet to assimilate or integrate. To put it another way, it's very hard to appreciate or enjoy any music, when three songs are playing at once over each other, and different groups keep insisting one song gets turned up higher, resulting in the other groups doing the same.

I often wonder if these same individuals would have the audacity to walk into a business in China, the middle east or an African country and declare that they'd like to see more European people employed, to reduce the racism that's clearly present? It might not be an exaggeration to say that those in the office may be inclined to consider if that individual has a mental health issue and perhaps needs care, or indeed they may be laughed out of the office entirely and told where to go not so politely.

CHAPTER 3

Gender & Race Quota

Grass roots of this idea began to emerge some time ago, with Hollywood being one with talk of things such as inclusion riders. This is the concept that the positions available be split into proportions relevant to gender and then race/ ethnicity. This is not a model aimed at achieving optimal performance, but achieving optimal inclusion.

To begin with, let us pose the genuine question of is this necessary? If it is the case that there are no actors, cameramen, sound engineers, make up professionals, etc., from a specific gender or what is deemed to be a minority group, then this would certainly equate to a major problem of racism or sexism. Yet in a world of individuals competing for potentially limited positions, simply pointing to a white actor or cameraman who is employed, is no proof that your lack of employment is racially based. As we have previously shown employers will favour the most highly qualified, experienced or competent applicant. Failing that there is the reality to consider that positions are not simply open and available all year round, this would be naive. The reality is that every year a large amount of educated or qualified individuals graduate from college or university. Each year the companies in question may only need a fraction of the newly graduated people, which inevitably leads to people being unemployed for at least a period of time. Often barring incompetence or a complaint against an individual, it is likely this individual will continue to hold the position in question for a number of years, perhaps even for life. Meaning that position in particular doesn't open up again for decades, all the while more graduates come to the workforce year after year. So it becomes easily recognisable, that in positions that are highly sought after there will almost certainly be a shortage of employment positions. As human nature is what it is, some will always seek to accuse external forces, when sometimes a simple reality is to blame. Consider how many potential actors are seeking a career in Hollywood, and how many of them may reach their goal. Yet with high profile actors of both genders and every race or ethnicity, it seems unlikely that those who fail will have been the victim of racism or sexism, yet there will inevitably be those who make the claim.

We are beginning to see a pattern I believe now of ideas that seem quite fair and implementable upon initial inspection, yet when we examine the application of these policies their projected outcomes often paint a picture worse than the one we're presently living in. Their seemingly virtuous motivations and goals descend into totalitarianism, and wreak of a big brother system that is far, far too involved in every aspect of our lives. Never in the history of democratic capitalist societies has there been talk of so much excessive involvement from the state in dictating employment policy, or indeed of enforcing identity politics and group identity based politics and policies.

The aim of this idea is that a workforce be more reflective of a society, which standing as an idea isolated without application it seems perfectly reasonable. Yet we will quickly find masses of people excluded, as fields of interest and desire fail to overlap perfectly with figures and percentage based allotments afforded to race or gender. For one thing must be certain in this circumstance, there cannot be employment quotas based on any parameters in one field, if they do not exist in all fields. That is to say it is nobody's right to demand a certain gender or race is entitled to a percentage based employment allotment in one industry, if they choose to ignore less favourable positions. It is not equality to demand women are 50% of newsreaders and TV personalities, without accepting that there must also then be a quota for 50% women in waste management and disposal, oil rigs at sea and mining companies. My point here being that nobody has the entitlement to cherry pick the glamorous and financially attractive positions, while imagining that nobody from their group will have to balance numbers out in another field.

This cannot be seen as anything but the agenda of incredibly self serving and naive people who have a deeper underlying agenda at play also. I say this due to the abhorrently hypocritical and ignorant entitled approach they have taken towards the issue. Theirs is a view ignorant to human nature and the desires of individuals, and they seek to crush society into a categorised identity format by which they can more easily assure themselves of their understanding of things.

It is essentially a racist view of the world, whether by intention or by confusion, and in many underlying ways amounts to a deep-rooted hatred of Europeans, and in particular men. As in essence a gender and race quota is tantamount to walking into an office and in layman's terms saying "Ummm could we get some women and non-whites in here please, ya know to reduce the racism?". So whether intentionally or not this policy has defined itself a target, the supposed enemy.

Let us examine the policy's application that we might understand it's plausibility, and it's potential outcome in terms of serving justice to equal opportunity. The United States of America is a standalone example of a truly diverse society, due to this it would not serve examination purposes to use such an isolated occurrence as a measuring guide. Let us instead imagine any other country vaguely on earth, in that it's population is compromised mainly of those who have been native to the land for generations, along with a small mix of individuals from potentially any and all nations, as we find most modern nations today will contain. Even in smaller countries, a few hundred thousand who are recently emigrated or are here through their parent or grandparent is relatively common. With this in mind we discover immediately that no one size fits all approach can be used, as varying demographics over individual countries would force a different percentage ratio to begin with. So immediately we know it will require quite some quantifying of populations. Secondly we will find that when a percentage of a populations quota is dispersed among all positions and professions, we may find ourselves travelling well and truly against the grain in terms of the nature of people. For example let us recall in northern and western Europe many Polish came to work and live for many years. Few people who had first-hand experience with this would dispute that a huge majority of polish who came worked in the construction industry. If there were gender and race quotas in play a great many polish might have found themselves unemployed. Due to being unable to work in construction due to their volume, or unwilling to take such positions allowed by the quota such as child minding, nursing, caring for the elderly or teaching to name a few.

A broader example of this might be to examine the case of individuals coming from countries with low literacy or varying education standards. Are we to expect that individuals coming from other countries will be nicely divided up equally into the career and job percentages we'd like to put them into? It would seem in fact that this policy will serve to possibly make it more difficult for people moving to a new country to secure employment. As it now becomes based on hoping that there aren't too many people of your colour, gender or culture already employed in the kind of employment you seek, in the country you're moving to, or you would find yourself having to accept a career change entirely.

Essentially the concept amounts subtly to totalitarian job monitoring. Insisting that each recognised group be afforded a fair or proportional split of available positions, whether they like it or not. This approach ignores entirely the shifting unpredictable demographics of career choice across different groups. There may be three years running where one group produces a majority of doctors, yet they cannot find employment due to their low quota allotments.

Then three years later the same group may be producing mainly engineering and technical graduates, as the random desires of large amounts of individuals year after year are impossible to quantify. Yet one thing is certainly naive, to imagine all groups will be conveniently divided into career allotment quotas naturally, and no individuals will face exclusion directly due to this policy, is quite apparently a mistruth.

There are also examples where a gender quota for example would force a terribly unnatural employment demographic. For example no individual with any experience with the industry, would dispute that childcare is overwhelmingly a female industry. Moreover I believe there are very few individuals who would complain about that fact, or like to see it changed. As presumptuous as it is, many would find themselves uncomfortable arriving to a day care centre with their child to be met by a team of 50% men. It is correct to note it is sexist to presume a man cannot care for a child as well as a woman. Yet I would argue that the uncomfortable truth is that many would rather not use that particular facility, and would instead opt to find day care with a team of entirely women. Though for a gender/race quota to be serving justice at all, it must be comprehensive across all industries and not simply desirable ones.

Then we come to the issue of the quota system potentially working against people. Whereby there may be an Asian woman applying for a position at Google. Let us imagine Google has already satisfied it's Asian female quota but not it's European female quota, due to a lack of applicants. We now find that Google would be unable to employ an Asian woman for a position they need filled, due to the requirement they hold a position should a European woman seeking that position come along. After all, the quota is the quota. So we're beginning to see how limited and restrictive this would prove as a policy. Yet beyond that I truly believe it may even add to unemployment. As misaligning figures of applicants and positions available failed to balance out, we may find individuals ostracised from their industry for many years more than would be the average waiting period.

This also fails to quantify the difference between percentage of overall population, and the percentage of graduates relative to the overall amount. For example, if black Americans should be entitled to 15percent of cameraman jobs for the sake of argument. Yet figures will prove that each year different proportions of groups qualified in different areas appear. For example one year it may well be 15percent of cameramen graduating are black, and the quota will work perfectly, presuming positions are available. Though in two years time black men may be the majority of those who qualified in that area, with very few others having shown interest that year. Obviously this will lead to a great many of then being simply unable to attain employment, not least when the cumulative effects of this policy are considered. In that the above example could repeat for four or five years before it begins balancing out again, creating an even larger problem created by the quota.

That is why in conclusion, I believe we should not stray from the principle of the best individual for the job, and all other factors should be ignored. To not ignore them, is in fact to lend extra weight or importance to race or gender, when surely the aim is the opposite and to eradicate it's relevance. So although measures should be taken to ensure racism, sexism or any other form of exclusion are not taking place, I believe it is relatively simple to see that forced inclusion will not be the answer, and will lead us toward as many, if not more issues. Another point often made is that surely one group cannot be held responsible for another groups lack of interest in certain industries? Should individuals seeking a career be punished numerically in their quota allowance to facilitate entry of individuals who do not desire entry to that field? Surely not.

In truth this policy equates entirely to creeping toward equality of outcome. Which as discussed is simply naively idealistic to ever occur organically in human society. In truth there is nowhere for a gender or race quota to hide when it is labelled quite rightly, as a subtle push for equality of outcome, without ever declaring its actual philosophy. This truly is a dangerously totalitarian view, that the state may interfere in the free market and industry of employment, in order to shape its proportions according to a misguided view of justice and human nature.

CHAPTER 4

Gender Wage Gap

To this conversation we could bring innumerable studies and surveys that could serve as evidence in many people's eyes. Again though there are discrepancies between reports, and these reports fail to quantify the numerous contributing factors. My aim is to contemplate the potential reasons for such an occurrence, and equally important, review suggested courses of action.

The issue is presented in such broad terms when given in view of cents on the dollar, comparing women's earnings relative to men's. The Gender Wage Gap is calculated including part-time workers, and bonuses, etc. This makes it easy to paint the wage discrepancy as an overbearing inequality, with no justifiable or rational explanation. It is wilfully and ignorantly presented as a scenario wherein every workplace or industry women are present; they are institutionally being discriminated against in their earnings. As we will venture to prove by common sense and critical examination, this is simply not the case and has been a gross misrepresentation of a truth being shaped into an inflammatory social matter.

Are men earning more than women collectively? Given the figures few dispute that to be true. Is it exclusive and there are no women earning more than men, thus implying the blatant presence of sexism? No, plenty of women earn far more than the average man. Are women in the same position as men being paid less? Yes, in cases, though that in itself is not proof or indication of sexism or a patriarchy at work, especially when there are, albeit less, women performing the same job as men who earn more. I would also argue that you can divide humans into any two groups and those groups will have a wage gap. We could compare young men and middle-aged men, women of the same age in different regions of a country or men and women of different nations and we will find there will be a wage gap present. Due to the many varying human interest and capitalistic factors I believe we could draw a line anywhere, compare earnings and find a wage gap. This agenda has been plucked and spun to suit a narrative with specific motivations which will be further discussed later.

The problem with figures showing men earn more than women is that they are simply figures, they overlook or fail to quantify so much of what is an important part of any earning equation. For instance, Jennifer Lawrence earned more than her male counterpart Chris Pratt in their film Passengers. Few people from either sex would have disputed that she was worth more to the movie as she was certainly the bigger household name at the time. If an income based gender wage gap is to stand as the proof of a patriarchy, then perhaps examples like this stand as proof against it? For if a patriarchy was in operation surely this couldn't have happened.

It appears many are indifferent to the simple realities of life. Some say without consideration "women should be paid the same as men!" To which I answer, which man? Do you believe all the male mechanics of the world are on an equal salary? Or is it possible that different companies pay varying amounts? Or that being self-employed might be more beneficial financially? So which mechanics wage do we chose to level up a female mechanics wage with? Assuming she is, in reality, being paid less. Then are we also planning to even out the male mechanics wages too so that nobody is earning more or less? In a nice equality of outcome big brother fashion.

A question the advocates of levelling the gender wage gap often seem entirely unconcerned with is, is there a male wage gap and a female wage gap? Would one man or woman being paid more than another not equate to discrimination? Only if a man earns more than a woman apparently is there foul play afoot. This I believe highlights the resentful nature of the movement. They show no concern for men earning less than each other, and are equally undisturbed if women earn less than each other. Its sole concern seems focused on singling out that some men earn more than some women, and that collectively the same appears to be true. Are we sure women performing the same job as each other are earning the same wage? If not, which there is no data to support the claim, then why is this movement so indifferent toward inequity among females in the workplace, or among males? It reveals the motivation and perceived enemy of the injustice, in the eyes of supporters of this idea, men all over the world in every industry. I raise this issue to draw attention to the fact that if a wage gap and equality were the true concerns of this movement, I imagine they could not have ignored these questions for so long. Yet with the narrative openly being the unconsidered vague statement of, women should be paid the same as men, we're left to wonder whether it is ignorance that causes them to be so one-sided, or merely misandric viewpoints. As the movement seeks to secure a result not arrived at organically through the capitalistic free market. It is undoubtedly equivalent to equality of outcome from a gender-based perspective.

Conscientious effort could have been discussed in the chapter on equality, but I believed it was becoming too long as it was. John Rawls is one of the recent most famous writers on social justice, and is known for being against the idea that an individual might deserve to earn more based on a natural talent of some kind. His viewpoint being that for example, Cristiano Ronaldo does not deserve a higher wage than anybody else, simply because he is far more talented at football. This talent is attributed to luck and genetic lottery, so Rawls would state he is no more deserving than anyone else, he simply got lucky as many may have worked equally hard but never achieved so much. However I believe his view perhaps failed to appreciate the value created by individuals such as Cristiano Ronaldo. It is due to their luck that they are able to entertain or provide value for so many spectators, yet is that a good enough reason to excuse the value they've created? Consider that the majority of citizens employed in some form of service industry, entertainment or consumable goods, will probably only service a few thousand people in a years work. Whereas in the case of a singer or athlete, they arguably provide a consumable product for millions of people each year. If a taxi driver was able to provide service to millions of people each year, he may well earn millions that year too. The fact he services far fewer people in his line of work per year, is the source of his wage never being even close to reflecting that of an athlete or entertainers. So in truth I believe it is a fallacy to believe the genetic lottery should not play a part in an individuals outcome, especially if those talents create massive value for millions of people. Rawls is also known to be sceptical of even attributing working harder to deserving a greater outcome, as he puts forth the idea that environmental factors may influence an individuals ability to apply themselves as others do. Hence even conscientious effort is not indicative of deserving more in his eyes. The majority of us would disagree I believe, though we see no issue with positive discrimination as described in the United States third level education system. The bonus point system certainly coincides with Rawls conclusion on conscientious effort, in that achieving the same score on the test is not required for certain groups, implying some are not required to work as hard as others. Rawls supposedly advocates for equality of opportunity over outcome, but to my mind removes far too much responsibility from the individual. How are we to gauge equality of opportunity, when we decide that not working hard enough to achieve your goal wasn't actually your fault, but the fault of the contributing factors outside of your control? That you somehow weren't afforded the same opportunity. Are we to then in the name of equality, agree that some individuals need not work as hard as others to achieve the same outcome? Surely this is too far removed from our current reality to be acceptable to people. To this extent Rawls is somewhat similar to Marx I believe, in that by removing personal responsibility he serves to create victim mentalities, as Marx's theory of historical class warfare would serve to discourage would be entrepreneurs. While Rawls' theory regarding conscientious effort can serve as an excuse to almost anyone for failure, after all, I didn't work hard enough because the factors around me prevented me, it's not my fault I didn't work hard enough. I do not claim to know why such intelligent writers did not see the disabling effect their theories might have on young individuals, but I feel these theories exhibit as I mention often, isolated thinking that has disregarded too much of human nature to remain viable. And despite Rawls claim to support equality of opportunity, it would appear his policy would actually be applied in an equality of outcome manner, as even not working hard enough can be excused in his eyes.

Allow me to make one of the most pertinent points relevant to this conversation. We live in societies based on capitalism, this is a good thing as most of us agree, unlike Rawls, that working harder deserves a greater outcome when compared with somebody who barely pulls their weight. Capitalism allows individuals who want to work harder to earn more. It allows companies to attract the high-level employees they seek by offering a better wage than their competitor. It is fair that somebody working harder deserves more. Yet when feminists advocate blindly and broadly that women should be paid the same as men, it undermines the very foundational principles of capitalism. We are not entitled to equal pay solely for turning up, we must be as productive as those we wish to earn the same as, if that proves the case we should certainly receive an equal compensation. Yet advocating to level wages regardless of productivity, value to the company or factoring years of experience, is going against what we as a society have believed for a long time. I am in no way implying that as a whole women have not worked as hard as men, I am merely highlighting that a gender wage gap makes no mention whatsoever or adjustment for contributing factors such as conscientious effort.

Let us momentarily examine the wage gap in the field of entrepreneurs. A great many entrepreneurs either barely remain afloat, or indeed fail within a few years. However those who succeed do not balance out the financial equation of those who fail, they vastly over-compensate for it. Losses accrued by those who have failed will be relatively small before throwing in the towel, while the many self-made millionaires and billionaires tilt the male entrepreneur category overwhelmingly into profit. Consider alone that Mark Zuckerberg's Facebook has cancelled out the financial failure of hundreds if not thousands of failed entrepreneurs, as many other gigantic companies have. This shows that given the male percentage of entrepreneurs is much higher, with immeasurable potential financial gain, we have no choice but to conclude that this alone massively shifts an averaged out gender wage gap. Indeed I have seen naive claims written stating that if a male entrepreneur and a female entrepreneur both have a hundred clients, that they should be earning relatively the same. This is entirely untrue, except in simplified industries with a set price. Consider both entrepreneurs were consultants. In this case the size of the client and the amount of work they require will vary from company to company, and to imagine simply having equal number of clients will equate to an equal earning is somewhat ignorant of the reality of the matter.

There are individuals far better equipped than myself who articulate the psychological and behavioural causes of such a societal phenomenon as a gender wage gap, having studied psychology for decades. Yet these are explanations that fall on deaf ears for those who refuse to accept any explanation other than patriarchy, misogyny and sexism. For the sake of avoiding confirmation bias I will not mention any names but implore the reader to investigate what is without a doubt a contributing factor in psychological and behavioural tendencies.

Many argue their concern is more specific, and relates to situations within a company where a man is being paid more than a woman for doing the same job. There are an extensive set of questions we must first ask before this alone equates to patriarchy, or even isolated sexism in a single business. Firstly there is the matter of seniority, as the basic policy in many companies is such that wages increase every few years to reflect time spent and experience gained, thus presumably making you more of an asset to that workplace. This may be a chief factor in the miscalculations of gender earnings to begin with. Yet we shall assume both arrived at the position around the same time, nullifying benefits one might have over the other due to experience or years spent earning for the business. Are their qualifications identical? Surely an employer would rather hire someone with a Phd over an individual with a two year degree, or no third level education at all. So we find qualifications or experience in the field previously with another company may affect earnings. Let us again presume that both new employees hold identical qualifications and experience, and started the position at the same time, which is often unlikely but for the sake of the argument we will presume it, nonetheless. We again presume that one employee doesn't hold a curriculum vitae with far more impressive and praising references over the other, also for the sake of the example. Lastly, we will presume it is not a physical labour based job such as a building site labourer or fireman, where it might be reasonable to expect that a man may have a higher output or endurance to keep work rate consistent than a woman. Assuming all factors are level, which in truth is highly unlikely, it is to my mind a rhetorical argument that both employees should be paid the same. Where value added to the company, productivity and skills which are treated as an asset to a company, are all equal, then it is reprehensible behaviour to pay one individual less than another, regardless of gender, race or any other factor.

However, I would argue this is almost never the case in truth, and the above factors come into play in the reality of the matter. Young people of both sexes may feel they deserve equal earnings to their older counterparts with similar qualifications. However, the reality is they do not have equal experience, thus implying the younger employees are yet to be of the same value to the business, as experience can prove invaluable. This would certainly be the case in many industries, healthcare, clerical or legal professions, construction or architecture, clinical psychology or teaching to name a few of the obvious ones. With this being a reality, we see men paid more than women in the same line of work, but also women are paid more than men in the same line of work, all based on the circumstantial factors not related to gender.

Productivity is also a major consideration for any employer, as productivity translates into value for the employer. To imagine an employer might not pay more productive employees a higher wage in the hopes of not losing them to competitors is arguably naive. Almost every business or entity in every industry or workplace has its competition, and one of the chief ways of competing is by securing the most competent and qualified individuals. Firstly, that they may acquire their talent and services, and secondly, that their competitor may not. With this in mind more productive individuals may earn more, attributed to their added value to the employer, as has been the case in capitalist societies almost everywhere. From a principle standpoint, few would argue that if they were to work harder than another they deserve more in return, and factoring this principle into the equation, makes this potential wage gap contributor entirely justifiable.

Perhaps the last contributing factor that will to many seem presumptuous, yet is a reality, is the topic of varying degrees of interest, based on gender. This is in reference to demographics of employment. We will likely find more male mechanics than we will women, as men are generally more interested in cars and machinery. While we will probably find far more women involved in fashion, clothing or child care, as women lean more toward these industries before they might consider a trade for a career. These are generalisations, although never entirely true, they are to the extent of a generalisation useful for a genuine contemplation of an issue such as this. There will always be exceptions and each generalisation is only true to a degree, though generalised interests of men and women certainly play a major role, and to ignore this is to disingenuously contemplate the matter. Men being the higher percentage in engineering, professional athletes and entrepreneurs certainly has an effect on a gender wage gap. Many other professions could be added to that list but I believe it is clear now that organic interests of individuals account for at least some of the Gender Wage Gap.

In conclusion, I am entirely in favour of equal pay for equal work, and I believe productivity, competence and skill sets should determine reward. However, I am certainly not in favour of blindly and broadly attempting to close a financial gap that has arguably occurred organically, and I resent the sexist accusatory nature of the movement and its ignorance to human nature and capitalism as a whole. Furthermore I reject its proposition of unjustly seeking to create a wage system that even communists would find shocking. For even Karl Marx said "from each according to his ability, to each according to his needs", meaning even he believed that equality of outcome was unnatural, and that need and contribution should dictate value.

CHAPTER 5

Gender

Here is a quandary so convoluted that some arguments on the topic are genuinely impermissible as coherent, intelligent debate. We will nonetheless venture to contemplate to a conclusion all of these viewpoints. I intend to contemplate from a neutral standpoint, but at the same time I will not give senseless notions more time than they are due. This may upset some readers as it goes against their beliefs, but I would remind everyone that the goal is to use critical thinking to dispel false notions, your lack of agreement with a thing not being true, will not make it true. I imagine some of these issues are so sensitive that no matter what is concluded, someone will be offended. That being the case, I will ignore feelings entirely and critically examine the issue from a logical perspective.

For those who argue the fallacy that we as humans invented gender, or that it is somehow a social construct, they have misunderstood the basic definition of the words they use. We did not invent gender, any more than we invented photosynthesis. It was present in nature and we labelled it, and tried to understand its relevance, mechanics or its purpose. In nature it would seem rhetorically obvious that the purpose of gender is to procreate, as gender and sexual reproduction is also the method used by most other life on this planet to continue its species existence. Since there is also no other way for humans to procreate naturally, we will indeed assume that for our species gender is necessary to reproduce naturally. I say naturally as of course we have developed the scientific method of artificial insemination, yet even this requires the product of the reproductive organs of each gender.

We as humans invented electricity, the light bulb and the boat, but we did not invent gravity, gender or the four seasons of weather. To label or discover is not to invent. To invent is to create something which was not in existence before you acted. It would seem rhetorical to most that before humans had contemplated their physical gender-based differences, most other life on this planet was operating on a gender-based, sexual reproductive system regardless of what humans had or hadn't figured out. As we were ourselves, again whether we understood fully or had labelled it or not.

If gender did not exist, then why would there be such a presence in media on how accepting and respecting a person's gender transition is so important? Moreover if gender is a social construct then surely the gender wage gap can be forgotten about entirely? These ideas run contrary to each other to a large degree, yet it seems no problem for those who advocate such ideas, to on the one hand speak of women's rights, yet on the other claim that gender is a social construct. It is easy to get lost in trying to piece together what some actually believe, aside from the complicated fact that a great many people believe a great many things.

Does wishing you were something make it so? If I really believe I am of a different race, then surely this is equally worthy of the status of individuals who believe they are gender free. There is no merit in affording people autonomy on the decision of their sex but not their race, etc. Surely if one is malleable then all would be, or none at all.

Height, sex and ethnicity, etc., are all features we use to differentiate ourselves from one another. I might be a 5ft 6 black woman, yet if I really believe I'm a 6ft 2 white man, can I be? Certainly by any clinical standard this is gender dysphoria, but where do we draw a line? Why would it be ok to change something as foundational as your gender, but not how I identify from a racial or cultural standpoint? Will we then perhaps tolerate those who choose to remain regressed mentally and emotionally, and see them as the 9-year-old they identify as? Or have we crossed the line now into a case where this individual needs clinical care? The problem with acceptance as a virtue is that it goes against its nature to draw a line; to say we will accept all of this but that is too far, is simply against its ideal. How long before there are those who try to deem paedophilia an acceptable sexual orientation? Or rape as simply a currently unacceptable fetish? Acceptance without restraint would be the unfurling of society as we know it.

For any who might ask why I've not made reference to the multitude of scientific evidence supporting gender, I would remind you that the intention of this work was not to be based on empirical evidence, but on reasoning and critical thinking solely. Again doing this would tilt the intended neutral standpoint of this contemplation to one of what might be deemed confirmation bias, although I would strongly disagree, as some information is so globally accepted that it is beyond the sphere of confirmation bias, it is simply fact. Nonetheless I will not draw on any specific science to prop up either view.

So then the question of is an individual entitled change their gender given that the medical procedure is now in existence? I would argue that to a large extent what one person wants to do with their body is of nobody else's concern, provided they are not harming anyone else physically or mentally, and they're not breaking laws of course. To that end I would say yes, an individual is entitled to undergo surgery if that is their desire. However I truly believe that this is a procedure that carries with it a moral obligation. That being of informing potential love interests. Although transition would be accepted it will most likely not be the preferable option for most people seeking a partner. It is unquestionably unfair to allow another individual to assume you are naturally the gender you portray, thus implying the type of future involving a family that most people seek. To undergo the transition from one sex to the other I believe requires utmost honestly with any potential partners, as I myself have no problem with people who want to transition, but I would be seeking a partner I could have a child with without the means of adoption. I believe I would feel betrayed and deceived if I found out later that this wouldn't be possible, and I had not been informed earlier. It is in essence a terrible dishonesty and deception, to disregard the fact that the overwhelming majority of individuals on earth are heterosexual and hence seek a compatible partner and relationship.

Yet as far as an individual's rights are concerned, I can see no reason why a person should be told they cannot undertake any surgery they can afford and desire, though I would implore the most serious of consideration to the gravity of the action beforehand. For I believe one should truly contemplate the reality of believing you were "supposed to be" the opposite gender. For there are many people who feel they were meant to be successful in one field or another, yet life was not as they imagined it. And feeling that you were meant to be a different gender, is actually somewhat impossible from a technical basis. Nobody was supposed to be anything in truth, not if "supposed to" is meant to imply a predetermined design. A child is simply conceived during sexual intercourse and the harsh truth is there is not one part of the child that was "supposed to be" anything, except exactly what they are born as. Parents may have wishes inclined toward particularly health, gender and potentially even intellect or talent, yet those wishes are simply the hopes of loving and optimistic parents, and again unfortunately they do not equate to any influencing or predetermining outcome as to how the child is "supposed to be". Even if it did, these would be the wishes of your parents and not necessarily in line with the gender you feel you're "supposed to be". So in truth I genuinely do not wish to be attacking or condescending, but I cannot conclude that the claim that anyone was "supposed to be" anything cannot be considered as anything other than a delusion. I do not seek to belittle or insult any individual, nor would I ever seek to ignore a persons suffering or personal circumstances of depression, or anything along those lines. But I can see nothing that would back the claim of any individual, that they were meant to be in nature anything but what they are. We were conceived and our cells began multiplying and forming to the end result of the baby we were, and the adult we now are. I may feel like I should have been 6ft tall and had a chance at a rugby career, but it is quite clear that I was not genetically intended to be 6ft.

Next we must ask can further genders be proclaimed in the future? If so how many individuals identifying as a new pronoun are required before you can become a recognised "marginalised" group? And is there an eventual limit to the amount of groups permitted? Or is it permissible that one day everyone feels so different that there are millions of groups, reflecting billions of people's nuanced identity features, as they see them? Which in reality would erase the group identities of race, ethnicity or nationality, and might erase the idea of a minority due to the population being so wholly divided that no clear majority is ever possible, due to no particular group being big enough to hold but a fraction of power. Potentially leading to the most civil unrest and infighting ever seen in a society allegedly enjoying peace time.

For the argument must be considered, if we are not free to create thousands upon thousands of new definitions and genders, then what has given the most recent iterations a privilege above any other? Demanding to be recognised in entirety to the extent of a passport categorization. Can there really be any science or logic backing one new gender that can't be made ten minutes later by another new one? At the risk of being repetitive I would again point out that the majority of other life in nature reproduces through sexual intercourse of opposite genders, or through asexual means. There is not one other form of life known to us to have a third, fourth or any amount of perceivable genders other than the original two. Yet the argument must be, we are free to create any number of genders, or we do not have the right to imagine any other than two. A middle ground approach limiting the amount of genders we can create would have to have scientific basis first confirming the new genders, and then discounting any new additions, which science certainly cannot claim to have in the slightest.

One of the last claims made by the advocates of gender fluidity that I feel must be addressed is that of the belief that the state should supplement transition operations for those desiring them. This seems a step too far immediately, as the state does not concern itself if I felt like I should have been 6ft, nor will it feel obliged to pay for leg lengthening operations should I undergo them to achieve the height I believe I should have been. This I believe is the correct course of action, as the floodgates would likely open on any other scenario. It might begin with state funded sex changes, and lead to all manner of cosmetic surgery being demanded under the same sense of entitlement. If I can have a free sex change then why not breast implants, a nose job or indeed hair transplants or hair removal? I group these operations together for one reason and one reason alone, they are all physical alteration operations, none of them are necessary for health or safety reasons, and the motivation for all of them springs from an unhappiness with your physical appearance. At the risk of sounding entirely heartless I feel I must assert, it is not the taxpayers responsibility to pay for any individuals self conscious or insecurity issues. If asked, we would most likely find that the overwhelming majority of people are not 100% happy with their physical appearance, yet none of us feel entitled that the state is obliged to bear the financial burden of rectifying these issues. Which after all if gender was invented and thus malleable, then there is no difference between the sexes. Then the desire to transition must be concluded as nothing more than the desire to appear entirely physically different to how one currently does. So in essence is not entirely different to demanding breast implants. Or genders are real, hence the desire to transition, but as I have said the feeling of this is how I was "supposed to be" is upon examination a fallacy. These individuals want to be a different gender, "supposed to be" is not a part of the equation as we've shown.

Lastly, a grave abuse to children is the allowance of hormone blockers, which are being prescribed by the medical industry to children who have decided they wish to be the opposite gender. In truth I place no small amount of blame on those parents who deem it acceptable to raise their children as gender fluid. This is enforcing their own beliefs upon an unsuspecting child, and I genuinely believe warrants intervention on the part of child services. Many medical professionals assert that you must develop genitalia initially to have the transitional procedure correctly, and that hormone blockers will leave individuals essentially in limbo. Having not developed their genders sexual organs, they now face being unable to transition to having the opposite genders sexual organs as a result, making their initial desire impossible through the misguidance of parent figures and medical professionals. Gender is not fluid or flexible, and to indoctrinate a child with this belief is a grave injustice.

With my own personal common-sense conclusion given I will reiterate that it is still my opinion that an individual's life is their own, to be lived unhindered by the opinions of others, again unless their actions prove illegal or of harm to others. To that end I believe it should remain an individual's right to transition from one gender to another, I would however advocate that like voting, driving a car and consuming alcohol, we enforce a minimum age requirement. And I believe it wholly important to understand the difference between accepting a thing, and promoting a thing, and where a misguided or incorrect approach may lead us in terms of consequences. With that said we move to the next chapter; Promotion versus Acceptance.

CHAPTER 6

Promotion versus Acceptance

In this chapter I wish to discuss a concept that may not be in the immediate vision of most today, but is all the same a most consequential issue, if handled incorrectly. It is the matter of crossing the fine line between accepting a thing and promoting a thing, and the inherent results of choosing incorrectly regarding certain matters. We have spoken on representation, which implies that any group recognised as a group, deserves its representation. It may be argued whether this should be directly proportional as we have somewhat previous, yet this is not what I intend to discuss. Instead, I intend to highlight the difference between acceptance and even the representation of a thing or group, as compared with the active promotion and encouragement of that same group or thing.

I believe we have concluded that individuals should enjoy the right to bodily autonomy, and should they wish and be capable of undertaking surgery then effectively it is none of my business. This section of society having representation in media and various other areas we can agree should be an entitlement. Yet as we are all entitled to become millionaires should we choose, it is often nowhere near this simple. Consumer industries are based on demand and supply, hence companies will rarely seek out acts that are not in demand by the majority, in fear of losing revenue due to a lack of appeal to the largest section of the market. This is not to say that any individual is being prevented from creating their own forms of representation or opportunities, it simply says that major companies will always chase the largest consumer block via what appeals to them. To this end, a percentage based representation will not be easily achieved in a consumer-driven capitalist society.

However promotion of a group identity particularly when it is a position solely invented for the purposes of inclusion, is now well beyond acceptance. Going beyond acceptance and inclusion is promotion, which essentially translates into encouragement. There are I believe several things we as a society should allow happen organically. I believe allowing young people to find their sexuality without one side being held up as special, is paramount to knowing we have not pushed young individuals in one direction or the other. Encouragement even when aimed at helping those who feel marginalised is an influencing factor that will decidedly have results. If this were not true parents would not encourage their children to be hard working, or encourage them to be mannerly and polite, or to play well with others. If encouragement bore no fruit we would have ceased it as a practise a long time ago. There are those who will argue this could have no effect on surrounding individuals, yet psychology has proven that the environment of an individual will indeed impact personality, which may manifest itself in any number of ways. The demonising or encouragement of any behaviour becomes a part of the environmentally processed framework of an individual, which in turn can have any effect from forming core beliefs and shaping personality, to instilling lifelong hatred or resentment in a person.

It is an outrageous proposition to tell a young person they may not vote, and cannot drink, but you can of course, change yourself from one gender to the other. To assume a child has this level of self-knowledge and vision toward the future is quite honestly naive and foolish. Thus to promote this issue to a child is perhaps not directly abuse, but certainly not acceptable behaviour, any more than telling young children how to use condoms or which alcoholic drinks are the strongest would be. There are certain issues which minors need have no knowledge of until they come to an appropriate age to contemplate. For let us be brutally honest, most of us will recall many things we thought we desired or wished to be as children, yet it is a rare case indeed a child genuinely knowing what they want from a young age. To argue against this reality is to be disingenuous.

We have concluded that the notion of gender fluidity or transition should not be promoted or offered to young children, then it would further imply that these issues are only advertised or promoted where appropriate. No parent can prevent their child from encountering the reality eventually that there are transsexual people, but there is little need to explain the decisions of individuals to transition gender needlessly early, due to their having seen something on TV or online prematurely. Children know nothing of most adult activities and to introduce them to them too early is tantamount to abuse and desensitising, which may lead to lifelong issues due to shock or trauma.

So then leaving underage individuals and their visibility of the world aside, should issues such as transgender representation be promoted elsewhere? As it was in the case of Caitlyn Jenner on time magazine. Let us consider it by the criteria of the earlier chapters subjects, for instance, percentage gender quota.

Presumably men who have transitioned to women can now avail of the coming women's quota in any industry and vice versa, it will remain to be seen if this creates a sense of begrudgement and screams of male privilege among pre-existing female employees, yet it appears, that would be how it functions. Fewer still claim to be neither gender, and among those claiming this stance a host of other genders or identifications have been simply thought up. We must ponder then in a quota system, is each self-proclaimed and defined gender entitled to its own percentage of positions? And what is to stop people abusing this by identifying as a gender to avail of its quota positions available? The question remains what to do when a quota, if proportionally percentage based, fails to secure a job for a minority group. For example, if in a small firm there are 23 positions available but one individuals identified gender is only .005% of the population. Clearly, .005% cannot equate to almost 4%, and this group will find themselves excluded yet again. If we are to configure the system differently and say every employer must hire, more if possible, but at least one of each minority recognised group. We will quickly find small business' such as convenience stores having to choose who to exclude, as with perhaps 5 positions available for example, it will be mathematically impossible to include all races, ethnicities and genders. While beforehand the method was simply hiring whoever best suited the position of all the applicants.

Moreover in the youth of society bandwagon behaviour and susceptibility are much higher than any other time in our lives. With an issue seemingly trending, as a society we risk pushing people who are unsure in a direction they may not have gone if it was not being glorified in a such a way, and may regret later.

The topic of those who have transitioned and now deeply regret the procedure is largely ignored and under publicised when the topic of gender arises. Those who advocate for legalisation, state assistance and promotion are happy to ignore the darker side of the issue. Equivalent to wanting a drug prescribed that works for a lot of people, and to hell with the people who were worse off as a result. Ironically applying a majority rules system to a specifically minority issue. Such is the hypocrisy of these theories they do not survive simulation whatsoever. Yet for a movement that paints itself as concerned with those victimised and marginalised, it appears indifferent to the victims of such a life-altering and questionably rational operation to be carried out. Most will know of the despicable tactic of conversion used in an attempt to convert homosexual people, and I would never advocate that those intent on a gender transition be forcefully dissuaded. I would argue that for those who are unsure, what may seem like supportive behaviour or encouragement may be pushing in the wrong direction which then leads to dire consequences. For as many profess honestly themselves, they believed a gender transition was the answer, but it wasn't. The operation did not solve any issues or serve to make them happier or more complete, and individuals report feeling equally lost and disillusioned with the world, merely technically another gender.

Is promotion against the idea of democracy? Democracy is majority rules, and from a majority standpoint to promote newly recognised minority genders who transitioned from one sex to another, will be unrelatable. Moreover it may force premature awkward conversations between children and parents, in issues a child's mind should not be contemplating.

Another example of promotion run amuck is the Instagram phenomenon of underage girls sexualising themselves in an attempt to gain followers, likes, and emulate women like the Kardashians. Were it not for years of females baring all on magazine covers in the name of liberation, the regularity of women being barely covered and sexualised would not have become so popular. It is largely done by those with status, which we know young girls will seek to emulate again and again. This only compounded the popularity of "liberation", as it now carried so much status performed by celebrities regularly. This promotion has inarguably led to the over-sexualisation of the youth today. As it is naive to argue that 14yo girls dressed the same 30 or 40 years ago as they do today. Adult women seem at times to be competing to be sexier than each other, while deeming their outfit cute, when it is inarguably revealing and aimed at being provocative. In an age of movements against female objectification, we find women are the chief perpetrators of self-objectification. As pouting selfies and posing scantily dressed to the world become the borderline norm of female behaviour online and in club settings. This level of repetitive, intentional sexual exposure to outright strangers, has never been the norm of our society until now. And I see no other attributing factors to its rise alongside promotion, other than perhaps the fashion industry which has undoubtedly had a major shift over the decades in its clothing design.

Another example of promotion having consequences would be smoking cigarettes. At the time tobacco went to market the health effects were unknown, hence similar to any another product they were marketed and promoted. The way in which they were promoted was no different to many other products, suggestibility and a sexual reference. Coca-Cola had its iconic bottle styled on the feminine form, while cigarette companies tried to portray their product as sexy and cool. It worked, as Kim Kardashian can attest, sex sells. The chief problem is that when you tell young people what they can't have they will be sure to want it, more-so if it was ever held up as cool, mature or sexy. Still years after promotion and advertising of cigarettes is illegal, and with the health risks printed on the packaging, a massive problem persists with young people taking up smoking, which has originated, evolved and grown from the original promotion and romanticising of smoking. I fear should we promote and celebrate the wrong issues excessively we will reap the consequences as a society of those choices.

The last example I feel should be mentioned is the history behind hemp, or marijuana as it's now called. With the state policy in the U.S of growing it prior to the slur campaign, and it's now gradual reintegration into medicinal practises, marijuana acts as a great example of how public opinion is shaped by promotion or slur campaigns, and how that opinion then has wide-reaching implications and effects on society. Before hemp became marijuana through demonising slur campaigns, it was widely seen in the United States in particular as highly useful. The paper industry among others felt threatened by hemps industriousness, and sought to rule it out as a form of competition through legal means. Although possible through corruption, reshaping the public opinion that it might not see the monopolising move for what it was, was necessary. To this end they branded it as marijuana in the media, and not only was it not useful, it was dangerous, or so the corporate-friendly media would have us believe. The fact it is being reintroduced into medicinal practise should serve as overwhelming proof against that theory. Yet its usefulness and the fact its paper output was far superior to a tree, were useless in the face of a mass demonising movement. This example demonstrates that engineered promotion will have profound effects, regardless of whether the facts support it, its omnipresence and repetition cause it to be more memorable than most other things, thus it enjoys a highly significant influence whenever enacted. Here the consequences were years of medicinal research into marijuana, that could have eased the suffering of many people. As many will know it is now used in varying cases from multiple sclerosis to epilepsy in children and has life-changing effects in terms of quality of life. For years society and individuals were deprived of this form of treatment due to the conspiring of greedy individuals and the excessive promotion of an incorrect idea.

Promotion versus Acceptance may be the most subtle and evasive topic to accept the gravity of the ramifications that come from threading the wrong side of the fine line. There is much talk and legislating of late on every individuals right to be accepted for who they are, and in turn not discriminated against. Which of course to any moral person sounds positively just. However, the line between promotion and acceptance is a dangerous one.

For instance the issue of gay couples and marriage is for the most part reaching a unanimous consensus among the western nations. That consensus being that it is perfectly acceptable and should enjoy the same relevant rights as heterosexual marriage. Most countries now allow marriage and have ceased discrimination against same-sex couples when it comes to issues such as inheritance, or property rights as a civil partnership. This is acceptance. There are those who would say that due to a minority of ignorant people that gay rights have not been fully accepted. I would assert that is incorrect, and that in life you will always find ignorant, disagreeable people. For instance there are plenty of people who break many laws, yet none of us worry that society has not accepted these laws. We understand that the law is the law and that some people choose to break it, regardless. Just as we accept gay individuals deserve the same rights and respect as any other individual, but some will perhaps refuse to give it, regardless.

However, we border into the territory of promotion when we start talking about having pride parades on school playgrounds, as is being done in England among other nations no doubt. The reason this is promotion and not acceptance, is by virtue of the fact that to have a parade is to celebrate, and to celebrate is to single something out. We celebrate our birthday because it is the "special" day of the year for us. We celebrate holidays or winning a prize or event, because it is a special time of year, or it was a special memory. The problem with celebrating one side and not the other is that when one side is celebrated it becomes the glorified side, which in turn can have a great influence on young impressionable children who may begin to wonder why through no fault of their own, they are not special while others are. In actuality this kind of parade creates the exact opposite of the kind of exclusion it fought against in the first place. By overly promoting and celebrating homosexuality, for young minds it becomes the reverse of the system which excluded homosexual people and their lifestyle from the public eye and media. The results were as we all know, a high level of depression in a community that felt it had to hide itself. I assure you the continued over promotion of a minority of people will prove to have an effect the lifestyle of the majority.

CHAPTER 7

Consent

#MeToo is a movement that few alive could have avoided hearing about in recent times. It is essentially a movement aimed at putting an end to sexual harassment wherever found, be it the workplace or in public. It originated and grabbed worldwide attention initially in Hollywood, but a great many advocates say it has been an ongoing problem in workplaces around the world. It is not an easy issue to discuss as many have heightened feelings about the matter, and its victims and perpetrators. Yet the danger it poses obliges us as adults to consider the implications with the seriousness they deserve.

What will its long-term effect on dating be? The topic of consent has become an incredibly dangerous development that threatens to reshape millenia of human courting and relationship mechanics. The proposition of this idea on the surface is not strange. Yet when truly examined it becomes a frightening formalising of what has for the overwhelming majority, been a natural and intimate process. Today consent has become a legal matter, and that in itself has without anyone taking notice changed the reality entirely.

Before the MeToo movement and the topic of consent, consent had been a silent mutual agreement between people. I would argue the vast majority of people alive today old enough to partake in sexual relations did so throughout the years under the age old system, of slow progressing steps with mutual, mostly non-verbal agreement. Arguably if you are unsure enough to ask for consent then you probably don't quite have it at the moment. I would argue that it has been extremely rare in human interaction that adults speak the words "will we agree to have sex now?" Or something along those lines. This is not the case, as getting to the point of intercourse usually involves going through a few stages of foreplay, etc. Then proceeding further from kissing or foreplay to intercourse, has always as I say been a silent mutual agreement, based on physical and non-physical signs of mutual enjoyment and willingness to proceed. This movement seeks to reinvent the manner by which we experience adult relations, by legalising and essentially contractualising the interpersonal relationships of individuals.

The reality is that we are ignoring entirely the subtle mechanism which we have operated under for thousands of years. Perceiving each other's willingness to continue further was the method by which we exchanged consent, and rather than giving consent verbally, it was the lack of consent that should be given verbally, or physically by pulling away indicating your wish to stop. In that you would know if you were kissing and you made an advance with your hand on a part of her body, often one of two or three responses clearly indicate what your partner desired. One is that your partner might put her hand on your hand, indicating that it's fine and she's enjoying it. Another might be that she may not move her hand, but keeps kissing you, again indicating she has no problem with it. Or thirdly, she may grab your arm or hand and pull it away, a clear indication and the verbalising of the words "stop" or "no" should be barely required. Or indeed she may just stop kissing you and tell you that she wants to stop. This is how people have progressed through intimate personal relations for as long as we have existed. Where if one was being too hasty, no or stop was the recognised objection, and it was no that was legally binding by the charge of rape. Now as we seek to change it entirely to being yes that is legally binding, it becomes another total opposite of what we know turning current ideas upside down completely. Surely men should be asked for consent too? Or that is sexism at work, though this is rarely a topic of conversation or a statement of intent for this movement.

Consider that when consent becomes a legal matter it requires the new and unusual form of written or verbal consent. Standing in front of a judge explaining that a woman was "giving you the eyes" and dancing with you flirtatiously, or that she grabbed your crotch while looking you directly in the eye and smiling, will be totally insufficient in the eyes of the law as consent, even if throughout the intercourse the woman never said no. If we're standing in a court of law, consent will require proof as evidence, to which we conclude it is likely only a written consent will serve as a proper defence. Given that verbal consent could be seen as given through intoxication or intimidation, and "vibes" certainly won't stand up in court, we find ourselves moving toward a definition of consent that requires written permission of a partner to engage in intercourse. If that won't kill the mood I'm not sure what will.

Are we to accept and agree with this reshaping and legalising of human interaction? What then of young people engaging in sexual intercourse who may not be old enough to write a legally permissible consent form due being underage? Are we to criminalise and charge both parties involved here for doing what humans have done for as long as we've existed? Or are we turning the courting of potential partners into a legal agreement that threatens to go wrong and ruin lives and careers at the drop of a hat?

With so much talk of equality, and this horrendously one-sided movement marching on doing its utmost to leave a trail of corpses and vacant job posts available to be filled by a gender quota. It has become difficult to believe hard line feminists have not weaponised a genuine issue in Hollywood, and decided to wreak havoc in some strange revenge for something an overwhelming majority of men did not do.

In my own country there was one such case of false allegation. To my mind this case was borderline rhetorical, and it was apparent that the woman in question was lying. When the accused was acquitted and the trial concluded, the accused went on to see his career destroyed in the coming weeks as a result, and his life changed by the type of allegation that never truly goes away. Yet the false accusers name is still unknown. This is a grievous injustice in my opinion. On a personal note I believe her name should be made public as I wholeheartedly believe every man deserves fair warning, and the opportunity to avoid this woman should they encounter her. It is wrong to protect a false accuser and afford her the opportunity to sabotage more innocent men's careers and lives. Men would likely want nothing to do with this woman with the knowledge she is liable to wake up the next morning and decide the sexual intercourse you had was now rape.

For legal reasons I cannot discuss the details to highlight how rhetorically false her claim was, but it was a genuine and serious injustice. Just as women or parents deserve to know if a rapist or paedophile is recently released from prison or lives in their vicinity, for their own safety, I believe men are entitled to the same warning of potentially dangerous women who they might unknowingly run into on a night out.

What then of false accusers being reprimanded to prevent the witch hunt we are currently seeing repeating itself? The Hollywood cases are seen as the flagship incidents on this topic as the world watches in disbelief at the unravelling of such a large scale of sexual harassment. I venture to say in Hollywood it appears there certainly is a systemic or institutional problem with sexual harassment. The casting couch had long been a spectre without confirmation until the many actresses and actors began to come forward. Though many of these cases are somewhat murky, since the victims stayed silent preferring to allow it to happen and receive the work, rather than report the incident and as they saw it potentially lose any chance at a career in Hollywood they had. It does not serve to excuse the initial behaviour, so regardless of the victims handling of the situation, it seems certain there is a problem in Hollywood with the expectancy to exchange sexual favours for movie roles. Individuals such as Corey Haim from The Lost Boys film, assert there is a problem with paedophilia also in Hollywood. This would serve to strengthen the notion that indeed, sexual exploitation of actors and actresses is occurring, and in larger volume than we wish to believe was true. However, the movie and music industry are arguably unique industries. I imagine the reason so much has gone unreported is the power these individuals hold. To be the one who decides which of the four girls who can sing is the one the label will sign, promote and turn into a star. Or which of the 6 perfectly good male actors will star in the next huge franchise, thus ensuring future work and a life changing opportunity. I put it before the reader that the power to change an individual's life so drastically, while perhaps threatening that there are a dozen more just like you waiting for the chance, is potentially the most powerful blackmailing tool human society has seen and brings with it enormous power that is open to abuse. The power to transform a middle class unknown actor or actress into a millionaire globe trotter, shooting movies and signing autographs for fans who adore you, might be enough to make a depraved mind believe he deserves sexual favours for such a life changing opportunity.

Once again when we ask if the issue of sexual harassment is systemic or institutional, I would reiterate that isolated events do not equate to a systematic problem, and cases of laws being broken do not imply the population as a whole have ceased accepting it as law. With hundreds of millions of women employed, and the current popularity of the MeToo movement, had there been millions of women harassed in the workplace then surely now is the time to come forward and be ensured that going against your boss won't get you fired as a reproach. As leaking that fact into the public arena will probably create a media storm. Yet we have not seen a massive onslaught or coming out of victims, at least not anywhere near a large enough scale to claim institutional sexism outside of Hollywood. In fact we have seen false allegations against men cleared, serving to damage the credibility of such a movement, as selfish vindictive women seek to use the movement to enact personal revenge or justice. Such is the power of accusation that has been handed modern women.

Virtue bullying and sexism have found their place in the consent/MeToo debate as well. Weaponised sexism has become a concern of late in the social and mainstream media platforms. Any man giving his opinion on this issue, inflammatory or not, is at once admonished for anything but utmost obedience or silence, in the form of being branded a misogynistic supporter of the patriarchy and thus a willing oppressor of women. Henry Cavill among other men found out the hard way that even a gentle constructive criticism is not welcome in the slightest. Moreover the Twitter brigade will be along following any such stating of opinions to fire endless ad hominem at you, while demanding you apologise for your reprehensible behaviour. The MeToo movement is painted as a women's struggle against oppressive, misogynistic men, yet it prefers not to differentiate between sexual assaulters and the great majority of innocent men. Thus any man in total agreement will be welcomed while anything other than full compliance will see you branded as part of the problem. Perhaps not a sexual harasser, but at minimum a protector of the patriarchy in their eyes. Again this serves as a convenient tactic to discredit opposition and imagine that you're holding the moral high ground. And we have seen with most of these issues logic is not a determining factor whatsoever in the face of blind allegiance to the accepted idea or philosophy.

This movement has brought with it a lot of buzz words and unfounded assertions, two of the most popular being rape culture and toxic masculinity. The lack of evidence to support a rape culture is only the beginning of the problem for such a baseless and ignorant assertion. Since it seems clear this accusation is not culture, in the sense of intellectual achievement, but culture in the sense of social behaviour or customs, let us examine if the claim has merit. For a rape culture to exist it would by definition of the word need to be a custom, or an encouraged or accepted behaviour. For example many countries have a drinking culture. It is not promoted that individuals underage consume alcohol, but it is somewhat accepted at a certain age as age appropriate behaviour. As generation after generation did the same thing, making it virtually customary and normalised behaviour with very little being done to counteract or try to stop it from happening. Now let us consider if this is the case with rape. It certainly is not promoted that rape is anything but highly illegal and reprehensible at any time. It is not socially accepted in any respect, and has never once been deemed as an age appropriate behaviour. Nor is there a legally accepted circumstance for rape, as with alcohol and minors as they approach being of legal age, implying that alcohol is merely temporarily illegal. Nor is it something that the vast majority of the youth have done, generation after generation, thus making it somewhat of an accepted customary rite of passage. To this extent we must conclude that if a rape culture exists, then the parameters for a definition of it, are unlike the definitions of all other cultures, such as a drinking culture or sporting culture. Which to my mind debunks the notion in its entirety as it fails to meet the criteria to be considered cultural. Nobody in their right mind disputes that a single incident of rape is one too many. But as the running theme has repeatedly suggested, incidents of reprehensible individuals committing crimes simply do not warrant the conclusion that the entire system is configured against your group. The figures, surrounding factors and relative information simply do not corroborate to a conclusion, or at least not the alleged conclusion.

There are feminists who advocate for consent for physical contact so strongly that they believe you are not entitled to change your baby's diaper, without consent. They truly believe, or this is one huge prank, that you should not touch your baby to change their diaper unless you both ask for and receive consent. Their stance presumably being that should you ask your child and given that they can't speak yet, should they begin to cry or give anything other than approval, perhaps in the form of a smile, then you are obliged to leave your baby in their own faeces until you have permission, or you are abusing your baby. This is how far removed from reality some advocates for this philosophy have become.

While related ideas such as toxic masculinity display an equal separation from reality, and in truth bear a serious undertone of sexist hatred. If we listen to those who assert its existence, they will rattle off bad behavioural traits they attribute to toxic masculinity, yet in truth have no grounding in gender whatsoever, and both sexes are equally capable of these kinds of behaviour. This is a sexist attempt to brand behaviour as worse than it truly is. For example if I were to be involved in an argument with a Chinese person and called him an ass, then he decides to call me racist. Of course nothing about what I called him implies a racial remark, but some seek to inflate incidents and mould them into a popular issue, which will endorse their victimhood. Toxic masculinity is no different, as it seeks to provide women the means of scolding men for any behaviour they may deem at any time to be toxic masculinity. For example, before a loud and confident guy was just a loud and confident guy, whereas now, he suffers from toxic masculinity. Another example is that young boys often play in a rough manner, this is age appropriate behaviour, and has been the norm possibly forever. It is the norm because just as women go through major hormonal changes during pregnancy, young boys go through a great deal of changes before,during and after puberty. One being that of learning to cope with their energy and testosterone levels, which are a part of our nature since before humans even had tools. Another example I have heard is that a man cutting across a woman while she is speaking is toxic masculinity, and indicative of entitlement to come before women. Although this may be the case in extremely rare situations, in truth this is a nonsense claim, as we cannot allow obnoxious or unmannerly behaviour to become branded as a male only problem, and all males disposition toward women. As stated this is a sexist claim and claims of a relative nature would surely never be tolerated. For example, if a woman got emotional on a topic during a debate, it is certainly not permissible for me to imagine that her toxic femininity needs to be kept in check while we have logical discourse. In all cases the claim is ridiculous as both genders are entirely capable of any behaviour, and to attribute a behavioural cause to gender rather than to the individual, is certainly a sexist conclusion.

CHAPTER 8

Abortion

For those allowing themselves to be overwhelmed by an appeal to emotion, and the minority cases of circumstantial suffering, these are often enough to warrant widespread policy change in their eyes. Their motivation comes from a place of genuine empathy, yet their empathy has overlooked and refused to acknowledge what was out of sight, out of mind. For in this debate there is a victim never heard from.

Let us examine what we can know. We know that for thousands of years in human history being pregnant meant there was a baby coming. In many cultures women are congratulated on confirmation they are expecting a child, as if they had already delivered and held the child in their arms. Such is the certainty and joy surrounding being pregnant in many cultures. We also recognise that no woman who is not pregnant has ever gone for a termination operation. Abortion is a procedure specifically performed on women who are sure they are pregnant, and no longer wish to be.
So we know pregnant implies the arrival of a new person. We know abortions are only performed on women who

know there is a baby arriving in a matter of months, and who have chosen that they no longer, or never wanted the child.

So the question that follows must be, does any individual have the right to abort a pregnancy that will almost certainly produce a new human life? When we know that a baby is likely arriving in months, do we have the right to intervene with that virtual certainty and execute the developing child in the womb? That we might avoid the responsibility, inconvenience or financial strain of having to raise that child?

Scientific arguments are often the anchor of many of both sides points of view. Whether it be that science confirms life begins at conception, or that the heart doesn't start to beat until weeks into the pregnancy. Though for the moment we will remove ourselves from these sources of information and contemplate the issue as if we were ignorant to the science of the issue beyond confirmation of pregnancy and abortion itself.

To discern between the two claims, one being that abortion is a human right, the other being it is murder, we must be sure the terms are being applied appropriately. We will begin with murder. Murder is described as the premeditated killing of one human being by another. A human being is described as a man, woman or child of the species Homo sapiens. As a rule of law, no significance is given to the age of a victim of murder. A murderer would not would receive a lesser sentence for murdering a pensioner than they might for killing a person in their twenties. Nor is there a lesser crime applied for murdering someone who might be terminally ill. The principle being that regardless of whether a victim had 60 years of life remaining or 6 months the murderer still has no right to cut another person's life short.

With abortion the person whose life would be cut short has no say whatsoever. Just as you or I had no say while our mothers were pregnant. We simply had to hope that our mothers had the moral fortitude to believe whether we were planned or convenient, affordable or not, they had created us and they understood it was their responsibility to give birth to us and raise us. Or at least give us the chance of being adopted and raised by other people, who want children but perhaps cannot have their own.

If the mothers life is at risk physically due to the pregnancy, then this rare case requires further scrutiny. How are we to justify protecting the unborn at the direct expense of its mother? The child is no less innocent than any other, yet we find ourselves facing an unimaginable choice of which is the lesser of two evils. Again simply thinking the issue through we conclude that should the mother survive, she might have another baby. Though should the pregnancy be continued, the child may survive without a mother. In situations so inconceivable I believe a woman or couple should be given the option to save the mothers life by aborting the baby. I consider it no less an injustice to the unborn, but it can somewhat be considered justified by the mothers life being saved. That she might be afforded the chance to try again also should she wish, or perhaps remain healthy to mother her existing children.

The above is one of the few exceptions I can rationalise that would prevent me from concluding abortion is totally and completely wrong. The other comes in the form of the grim topic of rape, which is again a genuine circumstantial minority of pregnancies. None of the rules have changed, and the baby is still entirely innocent, but it is again a case of contemplating the lesser of two evils. Many argue the baby should be carried to term and given up for adoption. In any situation other than rape I would be inclined to agree, though I believe it is too great a mental burden to carry to force a woman to give birth to a child that was conceived through rape. The multitude of physical and emotional changes of pregnancy are part of the process, though I feel it is too much of an after shock price to pay considering the victim has suffered more than anyone should already. In truth it is a no win scenario, similar to the womans health at risk due to the pregnancy, rape forces us to contemplate two choices that present no easy answer. Women who have been the victim of rape likely experience trauma or PTSD, and to force her to endure the hormonal and other changes of a pregnancy that she not only did not want, but reminds her of a traumatic incident, is possibly the greater of two evils.

However I do not prescribe the same sympathy and exception to people who have become pregnant without it being planned. It may still be an overwhelming change, and it may not have been what you wanted, but it is however your responsibility to not harm the life growing inside you. It is perfectly acceptable to give a child up for adoption if your circumstances or disposition warrant it to your mind. There are couples who cannot conceive naturally for one reason or another who are overjoyed to adopt a child. By terminating a pregnancy you not only end a life that was under way, and deprive yourself of your child, you also deprive a couple who would have been ecstatic to adopt or even foster your unwanted child. Although it may seem impossible, or it interferes perhaps with college or a career, these are entirely selfish reasons and do not constitute the right to end an inevitable growing child's life. The sole circumstance that should not be considered entirely selfish is financial. If the woman in question is certain she cannot afford to provide for the baby this can hardly be deemed selfish, as it's in consideration of the child, yet abortion still is not the answer. If the mother does not want the child, she should give birth and give the child up for adoption. Or if the woman would like to keep her child despite her financial circumstances, then I believe rather than the state supporting the termination of unborn babies, it should come to the financial aid of those mothers in need. After all, the government survives on tax, and every mother has a future citizen for the country in her arms. It is in everyone's interest in the long run they are cared for properly.

The medical consequences of abortion on the individual are extensive, and yet majorly swept under the rug which is a very curious policy to my mind, considering the implications and their gravity. Women who undergo an abortion are in fact at much higher risk to a myriad of health issues including breast cancer, low-weight or premature birth on their next child, being unable to deliver naturally and needing a caesarean section, or simply the onset of depression.

It should be of grave concern why the biological consequences of abortion are not more spoken of, considering the volume of conversation on abortion itself.

Yet those who advocate for it seem ignorant, or wilfully disingenuous concerning the likelihood of future medical difficulties for these would be mothers. It would seem their mistitled agenda pursuing human rights has little concern for the actual humans involved. Having lost their moral compass entirely, they assure themselves repeatedly that their cause is just and avoid any further reflection on the matter.

Consider China for a moment, where due to quite an opposite problem, namely overpopulation, the government enforced a one child only policy, while also allowing abortion. As many will know already, the effects of this were a gendercide of unborn females, with families favouring to have a boy to continue the family name in a one child state. This was blatant sexism as the deciding factor was based solely on gender, hence female pregnancies if healthy or not, affordable or planned, were aborted en masse. The problem however did not end here, as is known, China now has a problem with gender demographics. With I believe up to 10million men in the population imbalance. This may seem trivial compared to their overall population yet it has undoubtedly caused its problems. Consider there are now 10 million men in China with little prospect of having a life partner or family. They now face the lottery of trying to find love and a life partner in a numbers game configured against them, hoping they won't be one of millions growing old alone. It also had its consequences for existing women, as an already full public transport system now experiences sexual harassment cases, most argue largely due to what is likely a high level of sexual frustration as the gender field is so unbalanced. I imagine

Chinese women on a night out often encounter more male attention than they desire. Yet in a race to not be alone this is somewhat of an understandable behaviour on the men's part.

China's overpopulation problem is a long way from western abortion dynamics, yet I believe some of the same problems will occur, regardless. I give China as an example to demonstrate that even for overpopulation, abortion seems an unfit solution. For instance couples seeking to have one child may well adopt the Chinese approach and desire a boy to carry on the family name, which may well lead to aborting any female pregnancies until a male pregnancy is achieved. Which as mentioned, also encourages the likelihood of the woman experiencing health issues. This I believe is immoral, and somewhat akin to playing god trying to control the sex of your child, and is certainly a new phenomenon in human reproductive history.

Let us examine the further reaching consequential ripple effects of abortion being legalised in countries. To believe a change so monumental can take place to no effect is surely naive, as the vast majority of nations do not face India and China's population problem. Though it was my intention not to bring survey statistics into our conversation, I feel there is one figure that is too important to ignore. That is the fact that in countries where abortion is legal it has become so regular that 1 in every 3 pregnancies are aborted in some major cities, while the average appears to be more of a 1 in 5 ratio. To underestimate the consequences of deleting between 20% and 33% of the future population consistently will be catastrophic for any nation. Indisputably this is where we then run into the prevailing problem of demographic issues, otherwise often phrased as an ageing population. This creates a social issue as the next generation become too few to support the amount of elderly in the society. This is an egregious act of government as it does nothing but send the country into a downward spiral with no vision toward the future whatsoever. In my country of Ireland we have still not recovered our population numbers from before the time of the famine, in the 1800s. Yet our government of truly confused and manipulated people, seek to lower the indigenous demographic even further under the guise of human rights, while utterly oblivious to the effects it will have on the future of any nation.

Then they will call for more immigration, and the great replacement will be in full effect. As countries adopting abortion choose to suicide themselves slowly, and allow foreign nationals to become the future inheritors of a country, culture and history that is not theirs. Which will tie us nicely into the next chapter soon, mass immigration.

Many would argue that abortion was used as a demography control weapon, against the black population of the United States. This suggests that its creation was potentially to be weaponised, and aimed at convincing the "enemies" women to abort their children, thus culling their numbers. We might be wise to ask who is our enemy? Who may have put this in motion as our societies allegedly willingly use scientific population control, or demographic management on themselves.

Mildred Fay Jefferson once wrote that "abortionists have done more to get rid of generations and cripple others than all the years of slavery and lynching." She was not alone in her opinion, as many saw the legalising of abortion and placing of many planned parenthood centres in predominantly black areas, as a demographic assault and population control. Former Senator Mark Hatfield also spoke out, seeing abortion as "a form of genocide practised against blacks". Are we to be so naive as to believe the same weaponised demography tool is not being used on us by an unseen enemy? Perhaps we will conclude more surely after the next chapter.

Lastly, one is left to wonder what explanation can be mustered when these ideologues run into certain situations. For example, on the one hand there are hard-line feminists who say reproductive rights are a woman's issue, and that a man should have no vote. What happens then when an individual born a man transitions to being a woman, is this individual now entitled to a vote? Is it to be universally accepted this individual now has a right to speak on this topic due to a medical procedure and mental disposition? Do they have to right to an opinion prior to their physical transition? That is to say, if a man feels like he's actually a woman, but hasn't had the necessary operations as yet, is the mentality of identifying as a woman enough to qualify for a vote?

Obviously this is all nonsense, I highlight it to demonstrate that there are those who stand for ideological positions that are untenable, and have no real consistency in their beliefs. Nor do they possess insight regarding the quandaries of the future, as their inconsistent, fickle belief systems do not hold the substance to decipher a path of action.

Why is it nonsense in the first place? Well to suggest that any vote on any issue should happen under the guidelines of half of the population being oppressed of their vote, solely on the basis of sex, is nonsense. This would not only prove massively sexist and a step backward, it is also at a very foundational level completely undemocratic. The simplest of democratic principles is one that ratifies our equal rights by providing a vote for every individual of appropriate age; regardless of gender, race, religion, ethnicity, financial or social standing. To undermine that fundamental right is to begin unravelling modern civilisation itself, as the door swings open to any suggestion that there might be a justifiable reason why anyone might be deprived of a vote. This must be vehemently opposed as the covert attempt to shape and influence referendum outcomes and legislation that it clearly is.

Furthermore, I believe that anyone advocating such an idea cannot be involved in policy making, and we must remain wary of those who refuse to accept such basic rights, or who are unable to understand the importance of such an issue. With such people you will only encounter further irrational reasoning the more topics you raise with them, as they are in fact, precisely how they have been manipulated to be. Emotional, unreasonable and abandoning logic in favour of self-destructive, virtuous notions that they are involved in a struggle for civil liberties.

CHAPTER 9

Immigration

Yet another topic that has become almost inescapable is the media frenzy regarding the policies on mass migration. We will leave aside refugees for the moment, and discuss first the mass movement of people's throughout continents not attributed to war or civil unrest. I believe refugees are another matter as they do not fall under organic migration, but rather forced upon people, hence in many ways a separate issue.

The claim is often made, and often correct, that immigration serves to better the economy. Often providing personnel in areas where a community lacked in its own numbers, for instance, nurses or labourers. In my country for as long as I can remember there have been foreign nationals, specifically Chinese and Philippine people with Polish coming later, who arrived in manageable numbers and integrated as quickly as they arrived. One finds it difficult to argue that this somehow adversely affected the nation. However, I believe the major distinction between what has been happening and what is now happening, is the unprecedented scale of people now seeking to immigrate to western nations. Let us not be disingenuous and imagine it otherwise, what I have stated is the simple truth. There is no mass migration of people to Africa or Asia, the traffic is decidedly one way.

Let us examine the claim put forth by many that immigration is a human right, and nations seeking to control the flow of foreign nationals into their country must be racist or xenophobic. This to my mind is a ridiculous claim with no grounding in legislation or even common sense. It simply is not everyone's right to move to any country they wish. Each individual country owes us nothing, least of all the innate right to come live in their society, whether working or on welfare. To imagine otherwise is to allow ourselves to become entitled beyond belief, as we presumptuously conclude that we have worldwide rights to emigrate to anywhere we desire. This is simply not the case, as for example countries such as Australia and the United States do not permit people to enter their country without proof of employment, or a sum of cash. In the vicinity of 10 thousand dollars usually to ensure you can support yourself, and have not come to their country intent on claiming welfare. This is a reasonable approach as it should be obvious how quickly a nation will decline allowing hundreds of thousands or millions of individuals to flood through its gates and then crush its economy by claiming welfare. I would ask that readers recognise the simple facts. In my country for example social welfare amounts to 198 Euro per week. Now imagine we allow one million immigrants into the system without checking their employability levels, hence half of them end up on welfare. Consider that it will cost the government in the region of 100 million Euro per week in welfare payments, a tidy figure of around 5 billion Euro per year. Not to mention without work these individuals will need rent supplement to secure accommodation, in truth the final figure is likely to be three times that without exaggeration. So now we have seen a prominent argument against mass immigration. The economic, mathematical and common sense facts make it impossible for any economy to support so many outside individuals, nor is it any countries responsibility to provide such payments. Surely it is ridiculous to believe any single nation owes every human on the planet the right to live there, along with entitlement to welfare. We are each born in a nation, of which we are a citizen and hence entitled to certain benefits, but to imagine this applies internationally is quite innocent. I can imagine how well I would be received in Pakistan or Nigeria, had I moved there without employment, qualification or fluency in the national language, but believing I am entitled to payments from their government. I imagine the cries of entitlement would be loud and far reaching, yet we do not apply the same standards to others, which is hypocritical.

Is it not foolish to believe a nation can so suddenly raise its population by such a large percentage and expect that there won't be a shortage of the basics of life? For instance can we assume most countries have thousands upon thousands of homes just lying idle, waiting for people to come and claim them? This of course is ridiculous, and it is equally short sighted to assert that while most countries have an unemployment rate, there might be hundreds of thousands of jobs lying idle. If this were the case surely unemployment would no longer exist.

Contemplating such a large scale of migration it becomes naive to presume that large volumes of foreign nationals are arriving to their country of destination with an employable level of that country's national language. Arguably an employer cannot be expected to employ and pay individuals who are of little use to them given their inability to speak the native language.

So in reality we find should we allow mass migration to continue we will find ourselves with a housing crisis, our medical system and education system under more strain than it can handle, and the government's budget needing huge restructuring. The budget will need adjustment to cater for higher debt being incurred by the millions or indeed billions to pay rent allowance and welfare to those migrating who cannot find employment, or to tax the population harder to cover the deficit. In Ireland figures show approximately 35% of rent supplements in certain areas are going to foreign nationals. Ireland being a small nation recovering from a recession, I imagine the figure in countries like Germany, France or Sweden are higher.

This I believe to be an immoral course of action taken by our governments. It is inarguably wrong to expect a population to pay accommodation and welfare for hundreds of thousands of people who were not a part of the country in previous years. Given that the government's budget is largely composed of income tax, essentially this policy dictates that the taxpayer should bear the brunt of the deficit incurred. It is also the indigenous population that will feel the effects of perpetually rising house prices, as a constant influx of immigrants will serve to keep demand for housing high, while keeping the supply low. This of course is a delightful prospect for the banking collective and property developers, but a horrendous one for literally everyone else. This will inarguably also contribute to a rise in homelessness.

Furthermore, we should not underestimate its effect on democracy as we hand hundreds of thousands of votes to individuals who did not grow up in our country or culture. Who also may not carry our values and viewpoints of rights and society, and may inevitably cause civil war as the numbers of those opposed to our way of living rapidly rises. Thus changing our political landscapes forever, and essentially negating the indigenous peoples right to self determination via the democratic process, as masses of outsiders now influence their elections and referendums.

Then we come to the matter of education, for the most part Europe and the United States enjoy the highest levels of education. Are we to expect that employers accept lower standard qualifications when they are below the standard of the current environment? Anyone doubting this truth might ask why so many individuals from so many nations come to the west to study. It is because with certain qualifications you can walk into your field anywhere in the world.

The false presumption that huge amounts of immigrants coming to foreign countries will integrate seamlessly is also being proven to be incorrect. Many cities now see that when the numbers are low integration takes its course, and a change in society or anything related to it is unnoticeable. Though when the numbers are higher we see that these individuals naturally flock together to find people of similar culture, language and beliefs. This is being proven to lead to self-ostracised communities developing through no intention of malice, but through human nature. However, whether innocent in their creation or not, they pose problems to integration, as it serves to create a mini community within an existing one, that remains culturally isolated and strives to preserve life as it knew it prior to arriving.

These communities then shift the pre-existing political landscape. Modern politicians see themselves handed demands that previously did not exist, due to a new voting block being present which now seeks to move toward their original culture which they are unwilling to integrate away from. This is where mass immigration becomes immoral on the part of the ruling class that support it as it chips away at a system that only the outsiders coming in feel needs major restructuring. The very same political leaders who seek to invite the world to their country, are the same hoping to benefit from reshaping a political landscape, hopefully in their favour. Again this will prove untrue unless that politician will bend to the demands of the newly arrived culture block. Thus as mentioned creating dual cultures in which I believe consistency of either will be lost as they struggle against each other in every form from political to cultural and representationally.

It seems strange to my mind that a better solution could not be formed, as those who virtue bully are so programmed in their thoughts that any solution other than bringing millions of people into other countries is apparently invisible to them. Consider if you were an immigrant or refugee seeking to travel to Europe or the United States for a better life. What is it you would truly prefer? Particularly in the case of refugees it would be overwhelmingly so that rather than being told walk halfway across the earth to Europe and we'll help you, it would be unquestionably favourable to receive support in your country. It is likely most people do not wish to leave their home, I likely would not, yet they do so in search of a better standard of living or to avoid ongoing conflict.

We shall contemplate the circumstances currently in Syria as an example. Citizens are and have been fleeing Syria due to civil war, heading towards Europe hoping to find peace. If it were me, I would much rather the issues in my country were resolved, rather than having to move my entire family across the globe. At times I wonder what exactly is the purpose of the United Nations? If not to move into a country like Syria and help resolve the conflict. That the country might return to a state of peace and rebuilding sooner, thus stopping the flow of Syrians feeling forced to leave their lives and homes. It seems a far more intelligent course of action to allow the United Nations to deploy on peacekeeping terms, then perhaps financial aid can be supplied to the country that it might begin rebuilding itself. As opposed to the supposed virtuous notion that it poses no big problem for refugees to travel across multiple countries, and upon completion of their journey they will receive help. This is the cause of so many refugees of late losing their lives, that in our virtue we have told people seeking help "come to us, we're not coming to you".

One theory as to why this policy is adopted rather than offer assistance on location, is that our politicians prefer this policy, that they might gradually replace a voter population that has grown weary of their lies and failure.

Many parties have such tarnished reputations of late that vast swathes of the population will never vote for them again. How then are these parties to conspire to achieve votes and continue to challenge for, or hold power? This may appear far fetched, yet if we are to agree that aid within the country is preferable to forcing refugees to travel across multiple countries, then we conclude that our politicians either; A) have a hidden self-serving agenda, or B) are quite stupid and close minded in their attempts at resolving this circumstance. The term conspiracy has been subjected to slur campaigns and discrediting to the extent that anything labelled as such is considered a wild goose chase. Yet conspiracy merely implies individuals have conspired, which may well be the case here in my eyes. As the actions and philosophies of our leaders proves to be self-destructive and undoubtedly not in either peoples best interest.

We find that in reality we do developing countries no favours by contributing to the brain drain of their much needed human resources. It is unlikely that medical or education standards will rise while their best and brightest travel to more developed nations seeking better working and living conditions. To those who argue immigration is beneficial to the economy, this in truth is a selfish evaluation. As it may be beneficial to economies to receive well qualified individuals, but it does not benefit an economy to lose such human resources to other countries. Encouraging skilled migrants to come to our countries can only serve to dampen any development occurring in their own, which will ultimately continue the vicious cycle and drag out the eventual levelling of the playing field.

Immigration with the notion of diversity in mind will ultimately prove a fallacy, as it becomes akin to displaying non-indigenous peoples to signal your virtuous nature. Many may wonder how I could say such a thing, yet as we examine diversity its application becomes untenable and its motives quite suspect. Consider when a relatively small number of immigrants exist in a country, diversity of culture and peoples will not be maintained for very long. As the integrated population live among the generational nationals, we will find that inevitably over time they will marry into the native population. Thus to a large extent failing to maintain a quota of outside cultures and diversity. This leads us to the notion that only by promoting and actively working to encourage immigrants to come to our country perpetually can we maintain diversity of races and cultures within a society. Which brings us finally to the question, should we perpetually promote and seek migration to our country for no reason other than to display diversity? Which will over time dilute itself, along with the natives. Eventually creating countries filled with only mixed race individuals, which can only be seen as an overwhelming failure on the part of diversity, as it eradicates what it sought to promote.

CHAPTER 10

Racism

It is evident that the topic of racism is being examined more currently than it has probably ever been. Yet whether racism is genuinely more common than it has been, is a notion I am deeply unconvinced of. Let us begin by resolving the incorrect opinion that is being throw around, a redefining of a word that is not open to be redefined.

There are those preaching the foolish notion that only those in a position of power, influence or privilege are capable of racism. That it is somehow a behaviour linked with systematic power, and the oppression of those without. This, of course, is an utter lunacy. To anyone still coherent, racism should be recognised for what it is. To discriminate against or judge an individual with unfavourable bias based directly on their skin colour, or otherwise racially based features. There is nothing about power or wealth involved in racism. A poor person is just as capable of racism as a wealthy person, and contrary to popular delusions, every race is capable of racism toward one another. To determine the ability to be racist would rest exclusively on a persons social status is nonsensical, and an incorrect definition, nothing more. To conclude that only one race is capable of racism, is in itself, racism. The previous definition would leave poor people incapable of racism, which I am quite sure is a conclusion that would be intolerable.

So then we come to the question of is racism more prevalent today? If racism was on the rise then there would be more talk of it in the media, check! There is. If racism was more prevalent then most likely tourism and immigration numbers would suffer. I have not heard this complaint anywhere myself, or in the news or media. If anything, leaving refugees aside for the moment, tourism and immigration are seeing some of their highest numbers on record. So much so mass immigration has become a talking point for many of the world's leading countries. For tourism the same is true as the world experiences airline after airline of pilots going on strike, demanding not more pay, but more reasonable family oriented time off. Such simple demands as two days off together now and then to see their family, and not be merely sleeping between shifts. So it is fair to say immigration and tourism are at their heights.

I can only speak for myself, but let us be honest in our contemplation. I would never emigrate to a country where it was an issue that people of my colour might be discriminated against, few would. The prospect of racism overshadows any other aspect of attaining a better life, for most of us at least. If a nation was systematically racist then how could I ever succeed? Surviving is difficult enough in today's economy but certainly I could not thrive in a country racist toward my skin colour. I believe it would crush any prospect of achieving a better standard of living. However, millions of migrants clearly do not feel this is the case, or I imagine they would not be moving to our "racist" societies. In fact in many countries despite not being native to that country, you can avail of its welfare system, surely systematic racism would prevent any such thing.

Many may state it is precisely because of mass immigration we see a rise in incidents of racism, as the number of individuals of different races growing in a community may inevitably reveal closet racists that had nobody to hate until now, or so these individuals would have us believe. Again though I would draw attention to the strange fact of the numbers of individuals wanting to come to western nations still rising despite the media's loud cries of systemic racism. For example most will know of the unfolding situation regarding agricultural land in South Africa. I strongly believe no person of European descent would in their right mind move to South Africa right now. With alleged incidents of racism in the west receiving far more coverage in the media than the situation in South Africa, it would seem clear that if these individuals did not believe the news to be false, they would not come to western nations. For I would argue nobody moves to a country hoping the chaos will improve. As mentioned South Africa stands as a great example, but also we could ask why there is no stream of migration from these countries into countries like North Korea or Myanmar? Why is it the individuals wishing to move country are willing to heed the media and common knowledge warnings of travelling to countries such as these, yet seem to ignore the warnings of racism in western nations, and persist to flock here in great numbers? Surely this must be considered by any rational mind, for as I have stated I imagine there are no Europeans currently moving to South Africa.

Then we come briefly to tourism, which to believe is unaffected by the presence of racism in a society, is nonsensical. I have no desire to visit somewhere I might be treated differently due to my skin colour. I imagine it being very uncomfortable to live in a country configured this way, and even routine tasks like ordering lunch might create anxiety. Then with many other nations to choose from why I would select a racist destination is illogical to no end.

Cries of systematic racism become laughable when famous, rich and celebrated individuals of all colours can be found throughout a society. As is the case in most western countries. I do not wish to start making examples but one would imagine in a system that was racist Oprah could not have become what she has become? In fact systematic racism implies that there would be no individuals other than those indigenous to the racist system, who could have attained any measure of success whatsoever. Again this, of course, is not the reality of the situation, not even in the slightest.

To summarise, it is overwhelmingly unlikely that racism is more prevalent today, as today we see more successful people of every race and ethnicity than ever before in virtually every developed country. We may not find famous black rappers just yet in North Korea, but for the majority of the worlds countries race is not a barrier to success. Immigration and tourism figures are at their peak and this would be impossible if racism were as present in the world as the viewer seeking media would have us believe. Let us not forget these are business' and people who make their money by inflating issues to encourage the public to buy their product.

Why then does the media report as though it were an epidemic sprawling out worldwide attacking black and brown people? Well we're back to the simple age old motivator, profit. A controversial headline or front page has always sold more papers than say a sports headline or a moderate piece of news on government proceedings. The unfortunate truth is mainstream media will spin an issue any way they can, to make it sensational or shocking, thus appeal to people's sense of curiosity and their emotional response. The media have a history of printing a story of allegation that ruins someone's name publicly, yet they never exert the same energy when an individual's name is cleared, and seeks to have his innocence publicised with the same public effort he was deemed guilty. This is not the purpose of this chapter, however, it appears clear the media will need tighter legislation governing their detestable practise of sensationalising people's lives to feed their rapacious profit stream.

In truth, both mainstream and online media seek to inflate and exaggerate any act that is even debatable racism. Due to this we have college heads in the U.S holding marches for racist black women who attacked white men on video, while claiming they were attacked. The media have ensured the race card is the most popular card in the deck, and it has become blatantly obvious that many are eager and willing to have any excuse to use it. I do not care for political correctness, and I refuse to ignore my observations regardless of how unpopular they may be. It matters not as I feel an inherent duty as a responsible citizen to never shy away from difficult truths. Although generalising is a flawed and somewhat ignorant practise, refusing to acknowledge a blatant pattern, is in fact an equal if not a higher level of ignorance, and shrugging of societal responsibility.

I would like to address racism in the country of the United States of America. It is clear due to the size of the historic slave trade of north America it has a hugely different demographic to most countries. While at the same time harbouring a history of racism and no doubt a lot of Ill will toward certain hereditary groups. However as most learned when we were children, two wrongs will not make a right. I cite this because it would be sheer ignorance to overlook the fact that the racial hostility has changed direction, and become increasingly open on behalf of some black Americans.

Perhaps never in history have we seen so much racial hatred aimed at individuals who were not alive for the events in question. It strikes me as overwhelmingly childish and incredibly small of character, not to mention displaying an all encompassing ignorance to basic facts, clouded by pure unadulterated racism towards white people. I for one have no sympathy for anyone filled with hatred. I personally do not care whatsoever what is happening to you if your response is to indiscriminately hate innocent people young and old the world over. This is indisputably voracious racism going unchecked, due to an underlying media agenda and the movements of an enemy of the people moving in the shadows that we have yet to recognise and acknowledge.

The racism of this agendas footsoldiers carries with it the bizarre, untenable belief that their behaviour is somehow not racist. Despite them branding an entire race worldwide with the actions of a minority of its past generations, while at the same time utterly ignoring anything this group itself is doing. Never could I have imagined individuals would devolve into such ignorance to common sense, as we see emotion has overrun a section of society that now abstains from critical thinking or logic.

It is also quite naive to believe that the solution to racism is for you yourself to be racist in turn, imagining it will result in anything but inciting further hatred and racism in reciprocation. I wonder if some black Americans have envisaged that by being racist we will somehow all be friends in the end and reach peace? We conclude it is an immature victim outlook that has been installed, which seeks justice for events they were not a victim of, from people who were not alive to be involved in any way. There is nothing for this to be concluded as but raw ignorance and hatred based racially.

This, of course, is decidedly not politically correct, and an unpopular thing to say. To which I answer simply, I do not write for popularity; I write my observations regardless of whether they be considered flattering or disparaging. And since I am not a politician seeking re-election, I have no concern for being politically correct or offending potential voters.

We will move now to another part of the issue of racism, particularly in the media and in relation to the

United States. That is the epidemic of police shootings in America, particularly as shown to us by the media, shootings against black males. As I have said, I intend to speak on my observations truthfully and to examine the issue of racism in the modern day. To leave the issue of police shootings aside would have been to inadequately address the issue and potential contributing factors. One thing seems clear to most, that there certainly are far too many police shootings in the U.S. Yet as has been the style of this piece so far, I will not form an argument based on data, I would encourage the reader to do the basic math for themselves and arrive at their own conclusion. That math being to factor the percentage of crime committed by each race, versus the amount of men or women of that race being shot by police. The figures should prove relative proportionately if law enforcement officials are not factoring race into the equation. However if police in the U.S are indeed shooting black males at a greater rate, this will be evident in the over representation of their numbers in shootings, relative to crimes committed. The only guiding factor I would implore would be that the percentage of the overall population of a race, is not the correct figure to use. The percentage of crime perpetrated is the relative figure needed, as this is the true indicator of a particular races interaction with the law from a criminal standpoint.

Yet none would argue there are too many police shootings in the United States, and either the training system or the evaluation of personnel permitted to join certainly warrants scrutiny. Either the training entices a shoot first attitude, or there are a great many violent individuals being empowered to operate under a law enforcement badge.

However, when we discuss the issue of police shootings and are they racially based, we must examine the claim seriously. To be deemed race based systematically rather than the actions of an individual, there needs to be proof that the system, policy or training encourages this. Since there are many non-white police officers we will disregard this as a possibility. Were there racist motives in training or policy then surely a non-white trainee would have brought it to the public eye by now. We must bear in mind the fact that figures for police shootings encompass all races present in the police force. It would be a racist presumption to imagine all shootings are carried out by one race, any more than all crimes are.

We must also examine in cases of law enforcement shootings, regardless of race on either side, how many of the victims were armed, and or pointed the weapon in the direction of the officer, or indeed fired upon them. As I'm sure any individual will agree there is a certain amount of survival instinct about these situations. As an officer with your gun perhaps already aimed at an alleged criminal, if you see that individual draw a weapon and begin aiming toward you, at that point I would argue anyone's survival instinct will be to pull the trigger before the person in question had a chance to aim at you, and potentially shoot you.

In conclusion I see no evidence to suggest that the American police force is racist by nature or system. Though it has proven itself excessively violent, or in some cases overly willing to abuse a self defence scenario.

Then we must conclude that the claims of systemic or institutional racism are false. Unlike China where it is illegal to practise religion, thus making it systematic religious discrimination, as it is supported and encouraged by law. Or Israel's most recent legislation that serves to downgrade the status of up to 20% of its population. This again, due to being visibly supported by legislation is a genuine claim to systemic discrimination. Whereas many countries alleged to be racist fail to exhibit any of these signs that could support such accusations. Indeed the offences against the Jewish people's of Europe under Hitler's Germany were also systematic oppression. As is the push forward with legislation in South Africa to expropriate land from one race to another without compensation, this is certainly systematic racism and oppression as well. Indeed how women are treated in the middle east with regard to their rights, is institutional sexism as well. However western nations where allegedly racism is rampant, have systems exhibiting none of the above examples, traits of similarities. It is difficult then by comparison to equate actual systematic discrimination and oppression, with merely the accusations of such.

We do not worry people have not accepted other laws because of isolated incidents, but we worry people have not accepted laws against racism due to isolated incidents. We could as easily make a huge issue in the public eye of theft, which likely occurs far more often than racism, yet this is not the case, we do not worry society has not accepted the laws regarding theft. This makes it clear that along with the media seeking views and newspaper sales, this is nothing more than an issue that was plucked from many others and held up as a major problem. Why, will remain to be seen in the final chapter.

113

CHAPTER 11

Why You're Wrong

How is it that all of these simple misconceptions gained so much momentum so fast, without ever being truly examined? In this final chapter it is my intention to outline how, and why it is that so many people have been carried away by ideas that were perfectly palpable at a glance, yet under scrutiny become hideous misrepresentations of themselves. It is not by accident this has occurred on such a wide scale, yet I intend to show the manipulation and narratives which have carried them so far. And I assure you it is decidedly more simple than anyone could have imagined, when framed in the correct manner.

To begin with, almost all the proposed ideas we have discussed seemed very amicable initially. More to the point, they appeared to be rhetorical progressions of a just society, with many even feeling they were not before their time. Ideas and buzzwords such as Equality, Diversity and Gender Wage Gap, seemed like just and progressive ideas. While addressing issues such as Racism, Gender and Immigration/Refugees, appeared in the manner they were presented, to be the social issues that drastically needed a culture change, or a newer, more heartfelt approach. None of this however has happened by accident, as anyone who seeks to implement change often seeks to soften the hard edges and keep their policy statement as vague and appealing as possible, this has always been the case. Yet in this final chapter I will unveil many of the tactics of persuasion and manipulation employed by the advocates of these movements, in their attempt to misguide the masses and achieve their aims.

Firstly we must broach the tactic of appeal to emotion, and its goal to persuade via human emotions like empathy, or appealing to the very nature of humanity through displaying suffering. This is considered an appeal to emotion due to its disregard for other factors that might affect the circumstance, with its message being solely that of, suffering is taking place, and you must help put a stop to it. This is a virtuous notion albeit it an incredulously simplified one, that exhibits no signs of an actual solution but merely a call to action. A large part of the appeal to emotion tactic is the appeal to suffering method. This relies on the manipulation of the fact that when humans are presented with suffering, it automatically triggers their empathy. The people behind mass immigration hope that emotional override will cause you to ignore facts, realities and consequences, as many many people have done. They have been manipulated perfectly into carrying agendas that actually bite off their nose to spite their face. Yet the virtue signalling aspect coupled with all the appeal to emotion overloads those who do not have the fortitude of character to remain logical and consequential in the face of pure emotive influence and mass projection of an agenda.

However, the volume of suffering unfortunately does not create more jobs, homes or revenue. In fact a responsible individual finds that although the suffering taking place may be awful, we must consider if jumping off the cliff to save the guy who fell off is a clever decision or not on our part, and not entirely fruitless. Philosophy taught us thousands of years ago that we should not allow emotion to overrule logic, and abiding by that principle has been one of the major contributing factors to us ever coming this far.

The next major contributing tactic used was that of the appeal to authority. This is the notion that due to an individual being qualified or educated on a subject, that they are now the authority on that subject, and thus beyond reproach. This is often the case when a scientist or academic in a certain field and their work, are held up as confirmation bias that the theory or work in question must be correct. This of course makes no reference to conflicting theories held by equally qualified scientists or academics. And one seems to have little respect for the other lately as social sciences assert their beliefs regardless of scientific evidence against their ideas. Or again an individual studying women's studies might give no credence to the fact that psychology can prove that the mental disposition of men who rape is indeed different from that of the majority of men. This being relevant as it attests to the fact that there is no rape culture in existence, it simply is not psychologically plausible. Whereas narcissistic and ego driven individuals abusing their power time and time again, is and may always be a problem, and does not stand as proof of a grand gender-based conspiracy.

Another of the simplest tactics employed in today's information landscape is repetition, particularly effective when coming from different sources. For example you hear on the radio a conversation being had about the gender wage gap, then you pick up a newspaper and it's mentioned in there too about companies pay rates being looked into. Then a friend, family member or colleague brings it up because they've heard about it too. Then you head to YouTube and there are videos everywhere about it until subconsciously your mind has processed the repetition to the point you begin to think almost without questioning it, there really must be an oppressive gender wage Gap. Everyone's talking about it, surely they can't all be wrong? And to that effect I would deem this tactic as an appeal to acceptance through mass projection. If the media talks about it enough then it must be true, this has become our lazy attempt at keeping up to date with current affairs. Again, I am not disputing the existence of a gender wage gap, merely highlighting that the thought of there being one did not arise organically. It was crammed down everyone's throat until we accepted it, and from the beginning it was painted as proof of a patriarchy, and never once has there been a genuine attempt at a diagnosis or explanation. The call was immediately to close the gender wage gap and level wages.

A very new strategy I believe is that of virtue bullying. The ostracising of people everywhere who might not agree by deeming them morally inferior individuals. The idea that the only reason someone might disagree with you being they simply don't care enough to agree, or worse that they in fact carry hatred regarding the matter. One example would be that it seems anyone opposed to anything but limitless, entirely open borders, must be a racist or xenophobe, indeed Nazi is often the war-cry. This is an attempt to discredit the opposition's argument through ad hominem, by deeming the opposition as some form of reprehensible group, thus their opinion or viewpoint must be equally reprehensible and not worth considering. Ad hominem itself is not a new form of attack, however I believe the virtue bullying tactic is, and has evolved from what many called virtue signalling. It is a psychologically aimed attack at installing guilt for not feeling the same way the accuser does. Arguments such as "the borders should be open, these people just want a better life, why would you deny them that, are you some kind of racist?" Are aimed not only at over simplifying the matter in the first place, but then acting as though you are deficient in some moral or emotional quality that makes everyone come to the same conclusion, which concludes you must potentially be racist or xenophobic. Whereas perhaps calling you stupid or an asshole would not serve to illicit peer pressure from those around you, but it being shaped as you wanting to prevent someone having a better life, due to your bias? Well now you're really not coming off so well to anyone around you, and the social acceptance factor is now taking its psychological toll on the matter. It is a manipulative stance to take, painting themselves as holding the moral high ground and being on the side of the victim, while you're against that victim, thus not only are you wrong, but you should hardly be entertained.

Along with wild and baseless accusations of racism and xenophobia, etc. The equally baseless ad hominem attacks of sexist and misogynist are being all too lightly thrown around too. If we are to dispute any view point of a hard-line feminist we will be immediately branded as a misogynistic "mansplainer", who shouldn't be afforded any consideration when it comes to "women's issues". A sexist statement in itself. This attempt to silence opposing schools of thought is quite totalitarian in its nature. The aim is to simply discredit and silence any outside theories or criticisms, with effectively slur campaigns to ruin any credibility in the eyes of the ever important court of public opinion. Seemingly intentionally it seeks to be divisive as certain topics such as abortion become "women's issues", with a totally sexist disregard for the father of the child, without whom the child would not exist in the first place. Imagine circumcision was to become a "man's issue" and regardless of potential future medical revelations of benefits or consequences, it was to remain exclusively the father's decision. I imagine such an idea would not be welcomed.

Next is an issue which I believe wholeheartedly is wrong and should merit equal attention and punishment to sexual harassment or racism in the workplace. That is the financial ruin of those who disagree with popular policy or trending agendas. No doubt many of us have heard at least one example of men or women losing their job or career for speaking out against any of these topics. The Twitter social justice brigade often pays them and their employer a visit, and proceeds to apply pressure for the firing of said individual as a form of justice, justice for having an opinion. This has without any doubt created a culture of fear in the workplace, as any who might disagree with ideas such as diversity or quota systems are in no doubt that should he or she raise their concerns, they will as we've seen, be ostracised and likely fired. Which shows us that in an effort to increase tolerance and acceptance, we have in fact unleashed its opposite by reapplying blackballing strategies, and allowing the pressure and consequence based strategy of silencing free thought and speech.

Over-representation is another tactic employed the media, as they seek to make anyone who disagrees feel in no doubt that they are a bigoted minority. The chief aim being an appeal to popular opinion, thus implying the majority agree, leaving you to further doubt yourself due to you seemingly being vastly outnumbered. Forcing you to question yourself again and again, as you are anonymously painted as a tiny bigoted minority by both the media and fanatical supporters of the given policy. The goal of this misrepresentation is to make any individual opposed to the idea or policy feel as though there is little point resisting as the majority is against you, and will essentially enact the change without you. The effect on resistance this psychological tactic of enforcing a feeling of hopelessness can have cannot be underestimated, as it serves to dampen any will to resist or continue speaking out on the issue.

Social sciences and education have had their part to play in misleading the masses without a shadow of a doubt. It would appear many of the social sciences conclusions are Marxist in nature. Painting the population and society of humanity as a constant state of victim and oppressor. Often choosing to ignore facts and attribute any and all group success to the oppression of other groups, which of course is highly irrational and utterly ignorant to the facts. DaVinci did not oppress anyone when he drew the helicopter, nor did the Wright brothers as they invented the first aeroplane. Einstein, Shakespeare and Tesla I imagine also had not oppressed anyone during the course of their achievements. So although it makes sense to attribute the Roman empires rise and prestige to having plundered others lands, it is nonsensical to imagine events such as the renaissance or the many inventions or achievements of a group, arose directly correlating with the oppression of another. This is not to ignore that certainly empires have flourished by means of conquest. It would be certainly true for the Greeks, Romans, Egyptians, the Persians, the Mongols, the British and on the list could go. Yet again though isolated period based conquest is a very weak argument to support a groups entire achievements, moreover when the majority of any groups achievements will often prove to have been individual ventures, and not actually a group effort. The purpose of targeting the education stream of information, highlighting certain information while disregarding entirely other facts or schools of thought, is to indoctrinate the youth of society. This secures a huge voting block with a long life span for the advocates of these policies, and unfortunately it is quite easily accomplished. It is perhaps an offensive thing to say, but I believe it to be true in the majority of cases, the young people of any generation have very little experience of the world outside of classrooms. This lack of experience in handling the harsh truths and natural occurrences of life, leaves them much more accepting of a truly idealistic, yet unrealistic view of the world. Hence without perhaps having studied anyone else's work, or had very much real life experience or application of such theories, they are swept away by the well-framed notions of equality of outcome, or indeed Marxism.

So we have seen now the manipulative, morally pressure based conversion tactics of those who advocate these agendas. Hopefully I have also shown that these individuals do not stand on solid ground ideologically, as it is quite easy to paint them into a corner in which their policies are contradictory, incoherent and so badly thought out that they could never be applied without entirely replacing the ideologies we live by. They appear attractive at a glance until subjected to further scrutiny, at which point they reveal themselves as opposites to what most of us believe. I would argue with even a few hours thought most of these theories come apart entirely, and end up at war with each other, and yet there are those still aggressively asserting that they are the only way forward, unless you're a racist of course.

Now, allow me to present the reader with the final nail in the coffin of any doubt. I believe all chapters have been discussed sufficiently to be stand-alone arguments but allow me to frame the collective issues for what they truly are. You're wrong because in the 1920s Richard Coudenhove-Kalergi wrote the Kalergi plan. You're wrong because annually European leaders gather to present the Charlagmane prize to its winner, the first of whom was none other than Kalergi in 1950. You're wrong, because you have been too trusting and preoccupied. You're wrong because you do not see that these issues are not only connected, but quite sinister in their motive. Most importantly, you're wrong by design, as every one of these issues were engineered to be appealing aspects of your own self-destruction.

What was the Kalergi plan? What is the Charlemagne prize? Kalergi wrote that his vision for the future of Europe was one in which the Euro-Negroid, as he put it, was to be the future population of Europe. He theorised this could be accomplished through mass immigration of non-European populations into Europe, who would then ensure they had as many children as possible. His idea, alongside later developments encouraging the indigenous European population to slow its birth rates through a multitude of methods including abortion and promoting interracial relationships, would ensure that the European population would be turned into a minority and eventually replaced. To this extent that section of his writings are deemed the Kalergi plan, as it has become undeniably the aim of the current generation of politicians to implement his ideas that they now carry out in a systematic manner.

The methods of slowing birth rate mentioned are of course, women being consistently agitated to pursue longer, higher reaching careers, abortion, and the financial strain imposed on European families of late. Apart from the economic tide of booms and recessions, all of the above issues began post Kalergi plan. The financial pressure is no accident I assure you, as it coincides perfectly with ensuring European couples have as few children as possible. With that in mind, our leaders have no intention of ever trying to change the situation of the population.

The Charlemagne prize is given each year to whichever European has done the most work in the destruction of European peoples. No, you did not read that wrong. To many this may sound like a conspiracy theory, yet Kalergis writings are online for all to see and he was the first recipient of the prize. The ruling elite of Europe take great joy in receiving or attending the award ceremony. The ceremony for who has done the most in that year to manufacture the destruction of European population demographics under the deceptive term of integration and unification. With this considered, I believe we see clearly that the ruling class have been playing off a very different hymn sheet than the rest of us, for quite some time. I will not quote Kalergi, I do not see such a genocidal and racial minded figure as anyone worth quoting but I strongly implore all readers to research this truth for yourself.

Why does a dead man's plan have any relevance you might ask? Kalergi was the first man to receive the Charlemagne prize. This would indicate his ideas align with the purpose of the prize. Arguably, the prize may have been created specifically to award him, and to encourage the continuation of his work and plan. I will now summarise how and why each of the previous chapters topics tie into the Kalergi plan.

Equality is one of the most important pieces of the Kalergi plan puzzle. Without the belief that we are equal, it is likely mass immigration might never have come so far. Were it not for the liberal view that all cultures and people are alike, we may never have turned a blind eye to such a large volume of individuals of a different culture being transplanted into our home. Equality is a primary weapon in dislodging the European people from their own environment. Consider that without the movement of equality we are currently seeing, there may never have been talk of gender or race quotas, which of course benefit everyone except the European male. This is weaponised restructuring of the workplace, as without it, it is likely immigrants will struggle to compete effectively with individuals coming from the current society, with a higher standard of education and language skills. The ever so silent push toward equality of outcome also serves the agenda perfectly of being able to paint European people, or men specifically, as the oppressor. After all, how did you achieve your success or social standing if not through oppression? Don't tell me it was hard work, that's the oldest lie in the book!

Diversity essentially serves an identical purpose to Equality. Its promotion allows for the opening of conversation of quota systems in the workplace, government, etc. While attempting to pacify and actually make an indigenous population happy about the amount of foreign nationals being imported into their country.

Gender and Race Quotas again serve the purpose of dislodging as many European individuals from high paying or powerful positions as possible. Not only does this serve to weaken the financial position of the home population, thus ensuring most likely that they have fewer children. It also increases the social status of the non-European population, in the hopes this may make them more attractive to the European female population, to promote interracial relationships, as it is no secret that women are attracted to successful or powerful men.

Talks of a gender wage gap are yet another disingenuous attack aimed at painting men worldwide as the oppressors of women. Not only will this facilitate an equality of outcome based wage structure, which will silently kill capitalism, it serves the purpose of continually demonising successful men. Successful men in European countries are more likely to be European, hence European women are having their male counterparts painted as oppressive and exploitative, which again will serve to encourage interracial relationships, which is what the Kalergi plan is all about after all.

The concept of gender fluidity is possibly the most demonic of manifestations of the Kalergi plan. Its aim of course is to promote and encourage the largest possible number of transgender individuals in society, that it will lower birth rates. We find it is only western nations that are having the issue of gender transition forced upon them so ferociously by the media, third level education systems and our privately funded puppet politicians. This is in no small part attributed to the Kalergi plan and all those invested in it, which clearly include major media moguls and other private enterprises or Non Government Organisations.

The role of Promotion versus Acceptance I feel should be evident, as repetition is likely over time to make an individual more empathetic to a given issue. It also serves as mentioned earlier, to make people who might disagree feel as though they are a bigoted minority, serving to dampen future resistance to such issues. The role of both over promotion and the media in all forms can be seen clearly when pointed out, as all forms of media have taken to the over-promotion of interracial couples on screen or in advertising. The role of the media in all its forms is discussed further in the bonus chapter.

The role of consent in the Kalergi plan is of course, population control, coupled with the accusatory ability to destroy or remove individuals the agenda deems fit. It seeks not only to lessen the sexual activities between men and women, but also to fear monger young adults into steering clear of what will become potentially life changing situations if we allow consent to march forward. Most would agree that many children born, are carried by young mothers. With the penalty of law now overshadowing intimate encounters, this will again ensure that birth rates in western civilization fall, as again this is an issue solely based in western nations, pushed by private sources and western media. Indeed I have not heard the claim thus far but I do anticipate it soon, that non-European males cannot be held to the standard of consent because of course, they have different cultures, and it might be wrong of us to enforce our culture on others. At least this is the spin I imagine will be used to further distance European men from European women while facilitating the promotion of interracial relationships.

Abortion should need no explanation at this point. It not only annihilates a nations future demographic but also its potential future mothers, as women who undergo abortion are likely to suffer a variety of health issues as the years go by.

Immigration is of course the fulcrum point of the Kalergi plan, and without it arguably all other methods combined would be far too slow acting. Mass immigration coupled with African and Muslim birth rates being deliberately higher, is the single most effective method of achieving Kalergis aim of the Euro-Negroid and replacing European people entirely.

Among the recipients of the Charlemagne prize have been; Henry Kissinger, Former president of the European Commission Jacques Delors, former Prime Minister of England Tony Blair, Pope John Paul the second, former President of the United States of America Bill Clinton, President of the European Commission Jean-Claude Juncker, Chancellor of Germany Angela Merkel, Hermann Van Rompuy the former Prime Minister of Belgium and the first president of the European Council, and sitting French President Emmanuel Macron, to name a few. It is to my mind virtually inarguable that these individuals were given the Charlemagne prize in the same spirit Kalergi was given it, for their work on the eradication of European peoples demographic through mass immigration or other methods. For instance, Angela Merkel has allowed Germany's highest influx of immigration on record. Let us not forget to mention Nicolas Sarkozy, who served as President of France and effectively told his people to race mix with African populations or other methods may be pursued by the state. Let us hope that soon, the vile, repulsive and treasonous actions of these individuals will no longer go unpunished by the voting block. Leo Varadkar the Taoiseach of Ireland has stated his desire to see a million migrants brought to Ireland, an island of under 7 million people. It would seem clear to my eyes that our Leo has his eye on the Charlemagne prize for himself, and desires to place his trophy on his mantle. I believe these so called representatives should be ousted from any and all positions of power, importance or public representation.

Finally racisms role in all of this is to ensure that the non-Europeans being shipped en masse into Europe are beyond reproach. Any kind of highlighting of wrong doing or behavioural patterns is immediately dismissed as racism. This not only turns a blind eye to crime, it serves the purpose of ad hominem and branding of a racist, in the hopes of discrediting all potential future arguments you may bring forth.

Additionally I might add that the role of "toxic masculinity" in the Kalergi plan is to facilitate the perpetual demonisation of European males, while also pushing those of weaker character toward being pacified. It also facilitates the rise of children being raised gender-fluid, as we seek to rid toxic masculinity from our boys in society. Perhaps even contributing to the growing number of gender transitions, as young boys seek to escape a lifetime of open verbal discrimination from all sides, in the racist and sexist manner regarding their European male description.

To any reader who may feel I have made too big of a leap in concluding all of this, I would ask you to consider; if you were attempting to contribute to such a doctrine, what conclusions might you reach in terms of plausible methods to achieve such an outcome? No doubt immigration and interracial relationships must be a major cog in the wheel. Then comes the issue of justifying such large scale immigration. Surely the repetition of information that has been spun to serve its narrative would suffice. By this I refer to perpetual narrative in western nations of late, that we are all part of an ageing population which if not propped up by immigration will lead to ruin for everyone involved. Also the lie of a declining demographic being shaped as an organic problem, and not directly created by the constant coercion of women into the workforce, the systematic financial pressure applied to the majority of the population leading to affording fewer children, and of course, abortion. Abortion as a means of slowing birth rate will serve to propagate the lie that fertility is somehow lower in these countries, when in fact the pregnancy rates are much the same it is simply the birth and delivery rates that have dropped, as mentioned earlier up to 1 in 3 pregnancies in some cities will be terminated. If you are particularly creative, conniving and evil, you might even seek to muddy the water with subjects like gender, again knowing that any individual deciding to be transsexual is likely an individual who will not have children.

I understand there are a few who believe that race mixing is inevitable over time in a globalised world, and I would not dispute that. I would merely question the validity of the agenda of a man who is no longer with us and quite clearly saw humanity as some sort of board-game to be organised and controlled. Again I do not dispute that interracial relationships are bound to occur, it is not on this basis that I feel disgust toward Kalergis plan. No, it is more a case of relativity, as I imagine if Asian leadership decided tomorrow that they would like to make Asia more mixed their people would be none too happy about it. Were African leaders to subtly begin allowing mass migration of Caucasian or Asian peoples into Africa, again no doubt there would be worldwide cries of displacement. Yet as the media favour this agenda we find that rather than draw attention to this issue they in fact facilitate it by down-playing foreign national crime rates or refusing to mention details of perpetrators at all, and branding anyone highlighting such issues as racist in nature and motivation.

If a planet of mixed race individuals with no discernible racial groups is inevitable, then so be it. If it is the fate of humanity to mix until no recognisable race exists then why not allow it to happen organically? What I struggle to comprehend is the hurry these individuals appear to be in. Why is it so crucial that the elimination of the European people is done as quickly as humanly possible? And why are other races not being subjected to this accelerated race-mixing? One would be forgiven for concluding there must be a more sinister motivation behind this agenda, or individuals or groups who stand to benefit from the acceleration of such an agenda.

Let us not forget that the United States of America and countries like Canada are also considered largely European populated areas. We would be remiss to imagine the Kalergi plan applies only to Europe, as it seems more so the European peoples are the target rather than the continent. To this end we see in countries like the USA again interracial relationships are over-promoted and actively encouraged. Though with a resident black population there need not be immigrants shipped into the United States en masse, as the existing non-European population is presumably to be used to this end.

More worrying perhaps is the issue of how did a madman's writings continually remain so popular with the ruling politicians? Who are the financiers behind these individuals coming to power? And how in the world did not one other politician come forward to bring this fact to the peoples attention? The last question I believe brings us to the horrifying conclusion that is virtually none of our politicians can be trusted. I say this because either they knew and stayed silent, facilitating and allowing it to happen unchallenged. Or they were too inept to recognise what was unfolding under their noses. Either in my opinion are grounds for lifelong expulsion from public representation, for actions against the interests of the people and incompetence.

To my mind, to proclaim to hundreds of millions of people, well you'll all be mixed eventually so lets get it over with, can be considered equivalent to also proclaiming, well we're all going to die someday anyway so we might as well get it over with.

Then we must contemplate who in their right mind would work towards such a thing? Apart from the rhetorical of those already named, I ask in a hypothetical manner. Who is it that would seek to finance the continuation of such an agenda? As one would imagine politicians acting against their own peoples interest would have to be bought for a high price. Leaving us to wonder, who has declared themselves the demonic enemy of the peoples of European heritage?

If you remain unconvinced and feel there is insufficient evidence to validate these claims, I would ask that the reader afford me one final consideration. That being that acts of wrong doing whether legal or illegal have always been concealed by those perpetrating them, and to imagine that individuals involved in such a long-running and expansive agenda would not take care to leave no trace of their actions is surely naive. In truth I am surprised they are so bold as to award the Charlemagne prize to this day, knowing it inevitably leads back to Kalergi and his wild ideas.

I implore that all readers search online to verify the existence of the Charlemagne prize and the Kalergi plan, these are not theories, they are public domain information. Wikipedia displays record of all of the Charlemagne prize winners since its inception, and a Google search of the Kalergi plan will also not require extensive searching as there is plenty of material concerning it for all to see. All that remains to be asked is; are you willing to believe they're unconnected? And in turn, are all of the issues discussed in the preceding chapters organic in their creation? Or are their ferocious, intolerant and vengeful attitudes proof of an agenda with a specified target?

All of this, might be Why You're Wrong.

About the author

Diarmaid is 33 years of age and was born and currently lives in Ireland. Having begun to suffer from depression at an early age he acquired no third level education, making him essentially self-taught in all pursuits. Finding solace in newly sought knowledge of philosophy, history, music and reading the writings of some of history's brightest minds, he sustained himself through what he declares as the darkest part of his life through self-education and creative outlets. Why You're Wrong being his first title release, upcoming works include additional non-fiction titles, fiction, poetry and music releases.

DO YOU WANT THE BONUS CHAPTER?

Join the mailing list to receive the
bonus chapter not included in the book.
Visit TheHumanSpiritPublishing.com
and click the link to sign up.

Follow the author on Twitter @DOConarain

Voice your opinion in a comment on the website or rate the book on GoodReads.com!